COMPANY COURTESY

COMPANY COURTESY

An action plan for caring companies

Christopher Ward

Gower

First published in the UK in paperback in 1990 by
Gower Publishing Company Limited,
Gower House,
Croft Road,
Aldershot,
Hants GU11 3HR,
England

British Library Cataloguing in Publication Data

Ward, Christopher
    Company courtesy.
    1. Business firms. Public relations
    I. Title
    659.2

    ISBN 0–566–02886–7

Printed in Great Britain by
Billing & Sons Ltd, Worcester

If a man be gracious, and courteous to strangers, it shows he is a citizen of the world.

Francis Bacon (1561–1626)
Essays 13: Goodness
and Goodness of Nature

The greater man, the greater courtesy.

Alfred, Lord Tennyson (1809–1892)
The Idylls of the King
The Last Tournament

Courtesy is not dead — it has merely taken refuge in Great Britain.

Georges Duhamel
Observer
'Sayings of our Times'
31 May 1953

Courtesy is not dead in this country, but it has a glazed look in its eyes and shows signs of going into coma.

Edward Pearce
Sunday Times
'Home-grown bad manners'
4 October 1987

Contents

YOU AND YOUR CUSTOMERS

COURTESY CHECKLISTS

Preface

Are you often surprised how bad companies are at handling the public? Telephonists sound bored and unhelpful. Reception staff appear to care little about the company, and less about visitors. Letters are answered ineptly and late. Job applicants are ignored. Customers are treated arrogantly, as if they were at fault for complaining about bad service.

Early in 1986, Munro and Forster Public Relations, whose accounts include leading names in fashion, cosmetics, household goods and charitable services, commissioned me to develop material that would help their clients recognize these faults and put them right.

Any advice Munro and Forster gave had to be based on actual experience, so over the next few months I kept a log of my contacts, by letter, telephone, or visit, with over 100 companies big and small. From this log I extracted the 25 most common public relations faults, and presented these to Munro and Forster in the form of an alphabetical Company Courtesy Checklist. That was the germ of this book.

The checklist was outward looking, but it soon became clear to me that was only part of the story.

It is very unlikely that companies will treat their customers and clients with courtesy and consideration if they do not treat their staff in the same way.

Good public relations start inside the company with the quality of personal (manager/staff) relations. Companies and managers need practical advice on ways to improve both. *Company Courtesy* aims to meet that need.

Company Courtesy is an A–Z of public and personal relations. There are 106 sections — 66 concern you and your staff (personal relations), 40 concern you and your customers (public relations) — plus a diagnostic test to find out how courteous you are before you start reading, and at the end a set of courtesy checklists that all your staff can use.

This book is about people and how you handle them. It is practical, not theoretical.

Company courtesy is the human face of management.

Christopher Ward

No discourtesy is implied by the use of he/his rather than she/her throughout this book.

Company Courtesy concerns both sexes. Male references are not discriminatory.

How to use this book

There are 106 chapters in this book. Each one covers a different facet of your relationship with your staff or your relationship with your customers. Cumulatively they cover every aspect of company courtesy. But don't try to read them all at once.

Each chapter is designed to

- make you think
- provide material you can discuss with your staff and use as a basis for training
- suggest new ways of working with your staff or for your customers.

The first thing to do is to find out which chapters you need most.

Start with 'How courteous are you?' on page 3 and check your 'Courtesy Count' and your 'Courtesy Profile' with the diagnostic test on pages 5–10.

The answers you get wrong will show you where you need to start.

Then read the rest of the book, in any order.

Finally, read the 'Courtesy checklists' on pages 125–139. These offer you ready-made training summaries for your managers and staff. Copy and circulate them if you wish.

Company courtesy involves other people. So let everyone read this book. Don't keep it to yourself.

Introduction

Is courtesy an outdated and time-consuming irrelevance?

Managers who say confidently that people are their most important asset, and then ignore them, will fail.

Managers who say that 'the customer is king' and then ignore him, will fail.

Managers who do not realize that the way they treat their staff will be reflected in the way their staff treat their customers, will fail.

Growth and success are vital for the health of any company, but you must aim for growth and success *through people*, not as some impersonal, numerical ideal.

People cannot be manipulated, calculated or computed as easily as figures. They are complex creatures, and there is no single or simple formula for working with or for them.

This book explores over 100 ways in which you and your staff can improve the way in which you work with people inside and outside your company.

Courtesy is the all-embracing name for this interaction, but does not mean effete old-world charm, status-preserving chauvinistic mores, or bizarre forms of office etiquette.

Courtesy in all its forms is an action-plan for personal and public relations that will lead to growth and success.

How courteous are you?

Courtesy is an action plan for personal and public relations, but do you know how much action you need to take?

You may be confident that personal and public relations in your company are superlatively good, but you can't be sure unless you check. That means finding out for yourself, not relying on reports from other people: they may not even recognize the problem.

It is vital that you systematically probe and question how courteous your staff are. If you find them lacking, take steps to train them to act differently. And don't think one check is enough.

Check regularly to ensure that you identify and correct faults before your customers see them. Otherwise it's too late.

Use the diagnostic test on pages 5–10 to check your 'Courtesy Count.' The test contains 50 questions on how you treat your staff and how you treat your customers. (The answers are on page 9, but don't look at them yet.) Answer as honestly as you can. If you don't know, say so.

Your confidence is fully justified if you score 40 or more. A score of 25–40 suggests that there is room for improvement. A score below 25 is a sure sign that drastic action is required.

Whatever your score, check your 'Courtesy Profile'. What do you need to improve: the way you treat your staff (questions 1–25) or the way you treat your customers (questions 26–50)?

Every question in the diagnosis is linked to one of the following chapters. Build your action plan round the questions you answered incorrectly. Then use the rest of the book as a basis for courtesy training throughout your company. The 'Courtesy checklists' on pages 125–139 at the end of the book are designed to help you do this.

Your next steps are to:

- check your 'Courtesy Count'
- assess your 'Courtesy Profile'
- plan your courtesy training programme
- use every chapter in *Company Courtesy*
- summarize your training with 'Courtesy checklists'.

Check your courtesy count

1 Is aggressive
behaviour a virtue?   Yes ____ No ____ Don't know ____

2 Is an apology a sign of
weakness?   Yes ____ No ____ Don't know ____

3 Do you know your
staff's birthdays?   Yes ____ No ____

4 Is chauvinism only
male?   Yes ____ No ____ Don't know ____

5 Is counselling just
giving advice?   Yes ____ No ____ Don't know ____

6 Does delegation
motivate people?   Yes ____ No ____ Don't know ____

7 Do you have an up-to-
date company
handbook?   Yes ____ No ____

8 Do you worry about
the health of your
staff?   Yes ____ No ____

9 Is asking for help an
admission of defeat?   Yes ____ No ____ Don't know ____

10 Do you prepare a
personal induction
programme for every
new staff member?   Yes ____ No ____

11 Do you worry about
good manners?   Yes ____ No ____

12 Do you have too many
unproductive
meetings?   Yes ____ No ____ Don't know ____

13 Do you know what
motivates you?   Yes ____ No ____

14 Have you looked at your company notice-board in the last week?   Yes ＿＿ No ＿＿

15 Do all your managers have objectives?   Yes ＿＿ No ＿＿ Don't know ＿＿

16 Do you use first names throughout your company?   Yes ＿＿ No ＿＿

17 Can you measure the performance of all your staff?   Yes ＿＿ No ＿＿ Don't know ＿＿

18 Do you expect your staff to sort out their own personal problems?   Yes ＿＿ No ＿＿

19 Have you praised anybody in the last week?   Yes ＿＿ No ＿＿

20 Do your staff resent your reprimands?   Yes ＿＿ No ＿＿ Don't know ＿＿

21 Do you allow your secretary to sign letters herself?   Yes ＿＿ No ＿＿

22 Do you have a clear policy on smoking that everyone follows?   Yes ＿＿ No ＿＿

23 Is it important to be tactful?   Yes ＿＿ No ＿＿ Don't know ＿＿

24 Does untidiness matter?   Yes ＿＿ No ＿＿ Don't know ＿＿

25 Do you know all your staff by name?   Yes ＿＿ No ＿＿

26 Do you acknowledge all job applications?   Yes ＿＿ No ＿＿

27 Do you encourage your customers to contact your staff by name?   Yes ＿＿ No ＿＿

28 Does body language tell you anything?   Yes ＿＿ No ＿＿ Don't know ＿＿

6

29 Do your staff know in detail what your company does? Yes ___ No ___ Don't know ___

30 Do your customers need you more than you need them? Yes ___ No ___ Don't know ___

31 Have you ever read the letters sent out by your computer? Yes ___ No ___

32 Have you forgotten or been late for an appointment in the last month? Yes ___ No ___

33 Do you train your staff to handle enquiries efficiently? Yes ___ No ___ Don't know ___

34 Are you pleased with your performance at exhibitions? Yes ___ No ___ Don't know ___

35 Have you ever looked at your own faxed documents? Yes ___ No ___

36 Is your company application form the best of its kind? Yes ___ No ___ Don't know ___

37 Do your staff gossip in front of visitors? Yes ___ No ___ Don't know ___

38 Do all your staff maintain the human touch with all customers, all day? Yes ___ No ___ Don't know ___

39 Are your invoices designed with your customers in mind? Yes ___ No ___ Don't know ___

40 Do your staff know who does what in your company? Yes ___ No ___ Don't know ___

41 Do your staff know what products and services you offer? Yes ___ No ___ Don't know ___

7

42 Do your staff address
    all your customers by
    name?   Yes ___ No ___ Don't know ___
43 Do you leave public
    relations to public
    relations consultants?   Yes ___ No ___
44 Are you proud of the
    speed of your response
    to customer enquiries?   Yes ___ No ___
45 Does all your publicity
    invite a response?   Yes ___ No ___ Don't know ___
46 Does your reception
    area sell your
    company?   Yes ___ No ___ Don't know ___
47 Is your signature
    legible?   Yes ___ No ___
48 Does good spelling
    matter in your
    business?   Yes ___ No ___
49 Do you regard the
    telephone as the most
    important point of
    contact with your
    company?   Yes ___ No ___ Don't know ___
50 Do you train your staff
    to work for the benefit
    of the customer?   Yes ___ No ___ Don't know ___

Answers to 'check your courtesy count'

Score one mark for each of the following answers:

1	No	18	No	35	Yes
2	No	19	Yes	36	Yes
3	Yes	20	No	37	No
4	No	21	Yes	38	Yes
5	No	22	Yes	39	Yes
6	Yes	23	Yes	40	Yes
7	Yes	24	Yes	41	Yes
8	Yes	25	Yes	42	Yes
9	No	26	Yes	43	No
10	Yes	27	Yes	44	Yes
11	Yes	28	Yes	45	Yes
12	No	29	Yes	46	Yes
13	Yes	30	No	47	Yes
14	Yes	31	Yes	48	Yes
15	Yes	32	No	49	Yes
16	Yes	33	Yes	50	Yes
17	Yes	34	Yes		

The total number of marks is your Courtesy Count.

Now look at your 'Courtesy Profile'.

Enter your score for questions 1–25 with a horizontal line in the left-hand side of the box below.

Enter your score for questions 26–50 with a horizontal line in the right-hand side of the box below.

Who are you treating better, your staff or your customers?

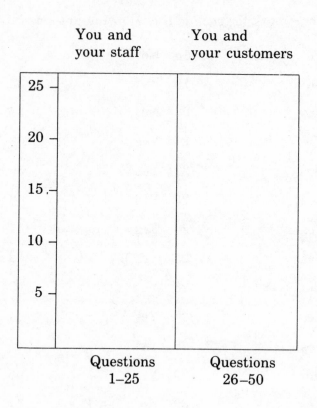

You and your staff

Aggression

Do you think aggressive behaviour is a virtue?

The Japanese find some Europeans 'aggressive', and many straight-talking, dynamic Western sales managers have been frustrated in their attempts to galvanize a Japanese sales force because of this.

The hard-hitting, pushy, single-minded approach, that may not seem at all aggressive to us, is offensive to the Japanese because it shows no respect for individuals and therefore runs counter to their canons of courtesy and good taste.

Aggressive tactics fail in Japan, but they will fail elsewhere for the very same reason.

To get the best out of people, you must show that you respect them, that you are capable of seeing the world from their point of view, and that you are willing to listen to their opinions and suggestions. This is courteous behaviour. To do otherwise is both discourteous and bad management.

Don't allow yourself or your staff to fall into the trap of believing that a macho management style is the way to motivate people. It does exactly the opposite. Aggression is rough, rude, and good managers always reject it.

Apologies

Is an apology a sign of weakness?

Everyone makes mistakes. They may be large or small, corporate or personal, but the biggest mistake of all is not to admit them.

This holds true at any level within a company, and throughout all its activities, but it is mistakes involving people that are the most difficult to come to terms with.

How often have you apportioned blame without investigating the facts, criticized too hastily, ignored success, been too busy to consider the personal problems of a member of your staff?

If you think you are blameless, you are almost certainly guilty of omission, if not commission, and the penalties are always greater.

Recognizing mistakes in personal relations is half the battle, but you won't win unless you take action to remedy them.

That's when you apologize.

Apologies must be genuine, offered in a supportive not a dismissive manner, and should be a prelude to some other suggestion that will completely heal the breach, real or imagined.

The aim of an apology is to build the team again. That's a sign of strength.

Appraisal

Do you and your staff set much value on appraisals?

A company's appraisal system is one of the most important weapons in its personal relations armoury. It is also the one most talked about, least understood, and frequently abused.

Everyone wants and deserves to know how well they are doing, and most people enjoy the opportunity to discuss their performance with their manager.

Why then does this meeting so often turn into an embarrassed confrontation where diffidence or perfunctory discussion replace the usual tenor of the relationship?

Why is appraisal so often considered a chore, to be accomplished in the shortest possible time, with no thought given to follow-up?

The answer to both these questions is lack of training and understanding:

- training in the reasons for and practicalities of appraisal;
- understanding of the deep psychological need and enormous motivational power of regular appraisals.

You cannot expect to get the best out of people unless you have some formal way of letting them know what you think of their performance to date, and what you expect of them in the future, of hearing their opinion of you, and of devising an action plan to make things better *on both sides*, which can be reviewed at the next appraisal.

Appraisal is a process of valuing and evaluation but is valueless if praise is missing.

Availability

Do you need a door to show that you have an open door policy?

Do you find that time-management seminars, self-discipline, an efficient secretary, and a carefully organized diary all conspire to prove that there are not enough hours in the day?

You can usually find ways of overcoming this problem so that the work gets done and your deadlines are met, but do you ever stop to think how selfish that is?

The people who miss out as a result of your over-full day are your staff. Do they feel you never have enough time to see them? If they don't complain it is probably because you are never there to be complained to.

Making yourself available to your staff by leaving your door open is desirable but not always the answer. It is frequently impractical, is open to abuse from time wasters, does not always encourage those who should make most use of it, and can lead to a belief that a closed door means subterfuge or crisis.

But you are failing in your responsibilities as a manager if you do not make yourself available to your staff at specific times of day, or by going to see them.

Walk through the office, warehouse, or factory floor, and let people see that you are interested in what they are doing, and are prepared to listen to them.

It is *you* who must be seen to be open, not the door.

Birthdays

Do you know your staff's birthdays?

Good personal relations need disciplines to ensure that you do not allow the mood of the moment or work pressures to affect the way you treat people.

Some people find this very easy and have no difficulty switching off their personal feelings or problems to concentrate on someone else.

Others find it much more difficult and gain a reputation for being moody, brusque, cold, or just rude. To its owner this reputation usually seems completely unfair, if not unrecognizable, but if it's what others see, it cannot and must not be denied.

There are a number of ways round this problem: a cheery greeting, an occasional drink, enquiries about the weekend or holiday. But these are usually fortuitous rather than planned, and may ignore those who have most need for this kind of reassuring personal contact.

One of the most effective ways of achieving informal, yet planned, guaranteed contact with your staff is to remember their birthday, and give them your good wishes personally on the day.

Don't make a song and dance about this, and don't let it look like an irritating duty. If you are likely to do either, it's better not to make the effort at all.

Your good wishes must be genuine.

Birthdays are each individual's unique anniversary. To acknowledge them is just one way of showing that you care about that person's uniqueness.

Change

Do you encourage your staff to change the way they work?

Every company should have an action plan for growth and success, but neither is guaranteed if people can look no further than the narrow confines of their job description.

The custom and practice of years may give people a deep sense of security, but this may well be at odds with your plan for better results, so something has to change.

Change in the way people do their job is the most difficult thing to introduce in any company, but it is easier if people can see why it is necessary. That means looking beyond and outside what they have been doing for years.

Sometimes it means a radical change in working practice, sometimes it means a reinterpretation, a new language, customer-focused rather than product or process-focused, to describe what they have always done.

The whingers, the workaholics, and the pessimists will all complain because they think their work is threatened. But you will need to teach them that work without tangible and beneficial results is pointless. The future of their work depends on results that are obvious to the customer.

Don't let work get in the way of change in your company.

Chauvinism

How many types of chauvinism are there in your company?

Answering this question may not be as easy as you think. You may not recognize some types of chauvinism because you are guilty of them yourself. Other types may be so subtle that they are recognizable only by those who are hurt.

Chauvinism comes in many forms. Male chauvinism will be the first on most lists, but it is not always the worst, or the most dangerous.

Female chauvinism can be equally damaging, as can the chauvinism of class, race, sexual habits, status, departments, education, training, travel, salary or bonuses.

Anything that causes one group or person to assume an importance they do not deserve, to the exclusion of others, must be prevented at all costs.

People are demotivated if they feel that they are rejected, ignored, or not thought worthy to be part of a particular group.

Any activity that leads to divisiveness of that kind is fatal in a company. It destroys morale, undermines authority, breaks down team work, and leads to snide infighting.

If your people can treat their colleagues, whom they meet every day, like that, think what they might do to your customers.

Clothes

Do you allow self-expression to take precedence over company image?

Clothes are a more complicated problem than most managers are willing to admit.

Few will recommend the Japanese egalitarianism of a corporate uniform, and most will reject a dictatorship of colour or style.

Your staff will also have strong views on this. Most will feel that what they wear is their affair and no one else's, and will reject out of hand any rules or guidelines.

The problem is usually viewed from the inside: what is acceptable within the company. This is wrong. It is what the outside world sees that is all important.

If your customers by their own dress and lifestyle show that they prefer jeans, sweatshirts and trainers, then anything else may be positively harmful to your business.

If your customers expect something more formal, then you should respond to this, and make your more informal staff appreciate why.

And why?

It is good manners to treat your customers in the way they most like to be treated. Clothes say more about your attitude to customers than you may care to admit.

If you can't stand the style, do *you* stay in the shop?

Communication

Is communication an art or a science?

Management conferences are built on it. Companies founder on it. Staff complain about it. Managers worry about it. Books are written about it. Consultants grow fat on it.

With so much being communicated about communication it is extraordinary that it still causes such problems.

But communication has become a science that is being destroyed by its own complexity.

Communication is human contact and the giving and receiving of information. We all communicate all the time. It's as natural as breathing. But in a business context it becomes an issue.

Courtesy is also about human contact and sharing. It involves putting the other person first, and thinking about what they would like rather than what you think they ought or what you can allow them to have.

The art, not the science, of communication is the same. What do people need to know to do their job better, to benefit the company, to make them feel good? What information will motivate them best?

And it is just as important for your staff to ask these questions: 'What does my manager need to know to help us/me best?'

Relax and think in human terms and the art of communication is as simple as breathing.

Worry about the science, and you'll need a life-support system that is devoid of human contact. Where's the communication then?

Confidentiality

Are secrets common knowledge in your company?

There are numerous forms of confidentiality: the sealed envelope, the rubber stamp, the closed door, the whisper, the 'private and confidential', the 'personal', the 'addressee only', and even the public 'between these four walls'.

Most of these are inadequate, frequently they are insulting, and usually they achieve the opposite effect. Leaks are the food of rumours.

Don't let confidentiality alienate when it is supposed to secure co-operation.

There are only two principles to be applied: the need to know, and the right to know.

Tell those who need to know, and they will use the information rather than merely divulge it.

Ask why others should not know. If you can't find a good reason, tell them also.

Openness is the best way of making sure that real secrets are kept.

Consultation

Is consultation a luxury or a necessity?

Consultants and the turgid wording of union agreements have tarnished the image of consultation by making it seem both more and less than it is.

Consultation is not a way of getting others to sort out your problems at a price that makes you realize you should be able to do it yourself.

Nor is it an obligatory way of passing on decisions under the guise of discussion.

Nor is it a process by which those consulted have the right to change or reject the issue that is presented to them.

It is a sharing of information for mutual benefit.

Consultation is the process by which staff and managers can help each other without loss of face or fear of censure.

It is the life-blood of an organization, and to ignore its importance can be fatal.

But do not let the name put you off. What's wrong with talking to people?

Counselling

Which is more important, the advice of the counsellor, or the decisions of the persons counselled?

To counsel someone needs training, time, sympathy, and skill, and if any one of these is lacking, it will fail.

Everybody has problems, or needs advice and guidance on what to do next. Yet rarely do organizations encourage staff to seek help. They often think they do, but do not realize that the 'This is how you do it ... so what's the problem' approach does not work.

Problems must be shared and a solution talked through so that it is arrived at by the person with the problem, not imposed by the person trying to help. This is true counselling, and is a fundamental part of the constructive management of people.

You must help your staff solve their own problems by acting as a probe and a catalyst, so that they see what to do next, confident in themselves that this is the right thing to do, confident also in your support.

You may pride yourself on the quality of your directors and managers, but how many of them are equally good as counsellors?

Criticism

Is criticism so critical that you avoid it at all costs?

No one likes it, yet it is frequently necessary. There is always room for improvement.

What is difficult is being able to criticize in such a way that people feel encouraged to improve.

All too often criticism is offered casually or intemperately with no attempt to share a point of view.

If you criticize you must also explain why you are doing so. To hear, accept and share the point of view of the critic is half the battle won.

A manager's role is not to tell people that they are wrong, but to help them see *why* they are wrong, and encourage them to operate in a different way in future.

It is very easy to find the right way to do this.

Just ask yourself what sort of criticism you are most willing to accept and why.

Why shouldn't others feel the same?

Culture

Does your company have a culture?

New chief executives frequently bemoan the lack of a company culture, then seek to impose one, and usually fail lamentably.

Managers fail to identify a company culture because they don't know where to look.

Yet a company's culture is its way of life.

Culture is created from within a company in response to forces outside it. It affects staff morale, management style, customer care, and executive drive. It is itself invisible, yet is one of the strongest corporate bonds.

If the culture is uncaring, lackadaisical, with no sense of a common aim, it will soon be obvious to customers that they are better off elsewhere.

If the culture is customer-focused, caring, dynamic and unified in concern for company success, then customers will want to share in the benefits this will bring them.

The culture of courtesy is the one culture you can see in operation, as it is the only one that binds customers and company together.

Delegation

Is delegation passing the buck or sharing the burden?

If managers merely pass on what they cannot do themselves, they will receive minimal support and scant respect. They will not even be managers.

The art of management lies in recognizing and respecting the skills of others, and using these skills to the full. You can't do this unless you delegate, using your skills to match person to task and task to person.

Delegation is a question of sharing and is one of the most powerful motivators of all, because everyone wants to be involved in the action, and to be valued for their contribution to it.

If you don't delegate, you give the impression that you do not value your staff or their skills. Have the courtesy to show them that you do.

And don't forget that delegation does not have to be downwards.

There is no finer example of shared activity than the occasion when your staff ask you to take on some task that they think your skills are better suited to than theirs.

Delegation is mutual motivation.

Dictation

Have you ever tried to write or type from your own dictation?

Dictation is one of those skills that is used by almost every manager almost every day, and because it is so common, is universally ignored.

Who ever heard of 'dictation training'? But how many secretaries are at this moment bemoaning the fact that not only is their boss incapable of composing a letter, but he can't dictate it either?

When did you last ask your secretary if the way you dictate suits her?

Do you dictate too fast or too slowly? Do you punctuate too much, too little, not at all, incorrectly? Do you indicate paragraphs, or do you leave that to her? Do you spell out unusual words or names? Do you tell her where to find any information that must be inserted? Do you take extra care when you have a new or temporary secretary? Do you remember to indicate the number of copies required, and the length and style before you start? Do you know when to stop?

Do you still expect your secretary to waste her time taking down your ramblings in shorthand? If so, just time yourself. How long does each letter take? Is this a sensible way of using her time? So what's wrong with audio typing?

Do your secretary the courtesy of dictating in a way that helps her to help you.

Expenses

Do expense claims bring on a character change?

It happens frequently. The liberal strategist becomes a nit-picking miser, and the small-minded bureaucrat takes the opportunity to sign away thousands.

And both will be heard to argue that expense claims are an irrelevance in the midst of the high stakes of corporate expansionism.

How wrong they are, but not for the reasons most people expect.

It is vital that staff are taught and encouraged to take a responsible attitude to expenses in the context of the budgets they control, and are trusted to do so.

Nit-picking, or its opposite, negates that trust and delegated responsibility, and can cause damage to morale and motivation that is worth far more than the small sums that were queried or ignored.

Expenses matter because trust is involved.

Trust is a valuable and expensive commodity that must not be squandered.

Face-saving

Is face something you believe is worth saving?

Saving face is not a concept much talked about in the West except among those travelling to Japan and other parts of the Far East. It is equally important here.

But don't make the mistake of thinking it is your face that must be saved. It is the other person's that matters.

An important management skill is the ability to criticize, advise, counsel, or help someone without taking away their confidence, motivation, or self-esteem.

This is true face-saving. It involves taking one step back to view each personal confrontation from the other person's point of view as well as your own. 'How would I feel in this situation?' 'What would make me feel encouraged rather than disheartened after this discussion?'

There is a type of manager who takes a perverse delight in bawling people out and then treading all over them. This is the opposite of face-saving. It produces short-term action, if any, and long-term resentment which is completely counter-productive.

If saving face is an introspective eastern concept, the outward looking western equivalent must be face investment. That will help your people grow.

Fairness

Are you as fair as you think you are?

We would all like to be considered firm but fair, the two characteristics most often cited as the key attributes of a good manager. But one is much easier than the other.

To be firm you must know what you want, why you want it, and explain this unequivocally to your staff.

To be fair you must also be prepared to see their point of view, and in discussion give this equal weight. Your staff must recognize that you have genuinely considered the situation from an angle other than your own.

This does not mean necessarily deviating from your own chosen course of action, but it does mean taking others with you because they recognize the validity of your argument.

All this takes time because you cannot be fair in a vacuum. Fairness depends on building a relationship, and having the courtesy to listen.

Handbook

After their first day, how often do your staff refer to your company handbook?

Every company goes through a phase of deciding that it must have a definitive handbook detailing its structure, systems and procedures. Everyone recognizes the need, but no one wants to be saddled with the task. Once done however it is forgotten, and managers sit back confident that the handbook exists but give no thought to whether it is still useful.

Company handbooks are usually long in planning, hasty in execution, and rarely used because they are almost immediately out of date.

New staff are given a copy and find it contains information and directives dated five years earlier. What sort of introduction to the company is that?

A company handbook is a vital tool but it must be designed to be used, and that means regular updating.

It should contain all the organizational information that everyone takes as read, and therefore must be read by new staff because no one bothers to pass such information on.

It should be designed to help staff communicate and do their job better. 'Who do I ask about...?' 'Where do I find...?' 'What happens if...?' 'Who is in charge of...?'

For the good of your customers, staff must have all company information to hand.

Handicaps

How easy is it for you to employ staff with some form of physical handicap?

Faced with this question, do you immediately think of ramps, lifts, lavatories and special equipment, or do you think about people?

The technical problems are usually the easiest to solve, and are a design feature of most modern office blocks. It is the personal issues (not problems) that need more time and care.

People with a physical handicap may need help to get settled into a new job, and to get round the building, but in the daily rush, how many of your staff would be prepared to give this help in a way that is pragmatic, genuine and uncondescending?

Most people have not come face to face with handicapped people and may have difficulty relating to them. This leads to extremes of behaviour from the blatantly rude, avoiding contact at all costs, to over-zealous patronizing.

Handicapped people are employed on their merits, not because of their handicap, and your staff must realize this.

Don't let the attitudes of your staff handicap the handicapped.

Health

Is your reaction to sudden staff illness irritation or concern?

You may well express the platitudes of concern, but your first thought was probably 'Just when I need that report finished today' or 'Now *I'll* have to go to Birmingham'.

Under pressure this is a natural, if selfish, reaction but it reflects a deeper problem. Managers do not give enough thought to the health of their staff.

Usually there is no need. Working conditions are good, and the occasional cold or stomach upset is par for the course. But you must not allow yourself to become complacent.

Not all health problems start and finish in the office. Genuine enquiries about the health of your staff and their families are important. And if the husband or wife is ill, why don't you send *them* flowers? It will boost the morale of both partners.

Don't let concern for the usual run of day-to-day illnesses make you oblivious to the more insidious forms of illness relating to stress. Stress takes many forms, and just because you thrive on it, does not mean that others do. Think about the pressure you are putting on others. Can they cope? If not, you need to do something about it before this turns into a more serious illness.

Often people do not want to bring such problems to their managers. Is there someone in your company to whom anyone can go easily to discuss health problems? If not, your company is likely to be an unhealthy place to work.

Help

Is asking for help an admission of defeat?

Some people think it is, and they never do. It is the responsibility of all managers to encourage their staff to ask for help without fear of censure or adverse comment. But this habit must start at the top.

How willing are you to help your immediate staff? Are you confident that they will come to you openly with a problem, or are they more likely to plough on regardless and make the worst of a bad job.

Openness of this kind has its penalties. A willingness to help should not be an encouragement for staff never to use their own initiative.

Productive help is to hear what the problem is, ask what solution is proposed, and support or question that. Don't let your staff think that you are there just to solve problems for them.

Train your managers and yourself to help people help themselves.

Induction

Is your induction programme merely a list of introductions?

It is one of the great ironies of business life that large amounts of time and money are spent on recruitment procedures and interviews, the best person is appointed, and then he/she is left to get on with it after a cursory programme of hasty introductions that is called an induction programme.

Staff normally survive in spite of this because they devise their own induction programme and very quickly find out what they want to know. But is that the right way to expect anyone to start?

Some companies produce an impressive induction checklist that covers everything from lavatories and petty cash to statutory sick pay and fire drill, but omits any mention of specifics that concern the new member of staff's actual job.

The induction process should be designed to help new members of staff find their feet as quickly as possible so that they can get on with what they were hired to do. It is a waste of their time and yours if they have to spend the first few days or weeks finding out by trial and error what everyone else knows but has not thought to tell them.

Make sure the induction programme is personal and professional, not just a tour of the lavatories and fire exits.

Interviews

Should an interview be an interrogation or a dialogue?

The numerous books that give advice to candidates on how to handle interviews usually mention that interviewers are often just as nervous as the candidates. What the books don't say is that most managers have had little or no training in how to conduct interviews and are not only nervous but just plain bad at it.

How many waste time asking the candidate questions that are already answered on his or her curriculum vitae or application form? How many have no idea what they want to get out of the interview, and therefore have no structure to their questions? How many talk too much? How many ask closed questions? How many have found candidates interviewing them for the information they want?

Applicants spend a lot of time preparing themselves for interviews. Don't you owe it to them and your company to do the same? What would you feel if you had prepared and dressed yourself for a dinner party, only to arrive and be offered sandwiches obviously left over from lunch?

Interviews are an inadequate and imprecise recruitment tool but they bring people together, albeit briefly and in tense circumstances. It must be your aim to make the most of that brief encounter so that a working relationship can show signs of developing.

Cold questions encourage cold answers. It is dialogue that reveals the real person on both sides, so prepare, relax and talk.

Involvement

Do you want your staff to feel involved in what you do?

There is a type of manager who sees organizational charts as a method of measuring the distance not defining the links between staff. It is that type who finds the concept of involvement threatening, and will do all he can to maintain that distance.

All business is a shared activity, and there is no possibility of getting the best out of your staff if they don't know what is going on, can't identify with it, and can't see what contribution they are making.

That's what involvement is. Your staff must have enough information to care about what they are doing because they see how it all fits in.

It is easy to exclude people by not passing on information. As soon as this happens, they feel alienated and demotivated because they can't see the patterns any more.

You rely on information to feel involved in your job. Make sure you involve others in the same way. It makes you feel good, it makes them feel good and it produces the goods.

Juniors

Are your junior staff just juniors?

When you think about your staff, do you think about them all, or only those who report directly to you?

Do your junior staff regard you as a distant figure or someone they can talk to easily?

There are many companies who rely extensively on the efficiency of their junior staff, but rarely admit it. The more the junior staff do, the more they are ignored.

To ignore junior staff is to ignore potential, and to run the risk that something will go wrong that could jeopardize your whole enterprise.

Junior staff, like everyone else, must understand what your business is all about, and why their contribution is important.

Encourage them to ask questions, make suggestions, and say when they need help, and above all talk to them.

If you show you care, juniors become people with names, personalities and potential that can be used in more ways than might be expected. That's how people grow.

Language

How often do you watch your language?

If you did, what would you see? An extraordinary mixture of mild obscenity, jargon, exaggeration, flatulent expressions, clichés, and vagueness.

Not only is such a list the usual mix of a day's conversations, but it is alarming and embarrassing that it is so normal, and delivered unconsciously.

It is remarkable that those who pride themselves on their business acumen frequently pay little attention to the way they express themselves. They either fail to get their point across, or alienate those they are talking to by using language that is inappropriate to the occasion.

All forms of expression are an integral part of good manners. To express yourself clearly, concisely, using language that is appropriate to your audience, is an essential part of good communication.

The language you use is meant to help people to understand what you want to say. If it does the opposite, what's the point of opening your mouth?

40

Listening

Are you and your managers good listeners?

It is a common mistake to regard listening as a passive occupation that needs no skills, something anyone can do.

On the other hand, how often have you heard the complaint 'He wasn't really listening' or 'He didn't really hear what I was saying'?

Don't underestimate the skill needed to listen well. It is a vital part of the communication mix.

Listening requires concentration, an open mind, sympathy, time, and the politeness to make it genuinely clear that you have taken notice of what people have to say to you.

Listening also calls for a good memory. There is nothing worse than listening well, only to forget and then hear the cry 'But I told you that on Tuesday'.

If you have difficulty listening and remembering, take notes. It shows concern and professionalism and people will respect you for it. What's more they will follow your example.

Beware of the manager who is all ears; he's usually deaf.

Loyalty

Do your staff regard loyalty as an outdated virtue?

When two or three members of staff are gathered together, loyalty and enthusiasm are usually notable by their absence.

Loyalty is one of those things that nobody talks about but everyone expects, though some may wonder if it has any place at all in a world of self-seeking entrepreneurs.

Loyalty needs to be talked about to emphasize its value at all levels from the corporate to the personal.

If you care about the people you work with, you do not spread their secrets, you do not complain about their inadequacies, you do not discuss their finances, you do not betray them.

What applies to your colleagues applies equally to the company itself.

How often have you heard shop assistants or receptionists complaining about their job as they offer to help you? What impression does that give of the company?

Loyalty is not a weakness of those who can't stand on their own feet. It is an essential ingredient of successful corporate life.

Manners

Do good manners contribute anything to good business?

Good manners are often thought to be irrelevant in today's business world because they show a concern for the other person which is at odds with a desire to gain a competitive edge.

Good manners therefore get a bad press and are looked on as a sign of weakness.

Yet we are all quick to notice and comment on bad manners, discourtesy and boorish behaviour, so why the antipathy to the positive opposite?

The reason is that few of us are very good at putting others first. Society no longer imposes a precise code of good manners on us, so we become careless in our behaviour towards others.

Good manners require effort, and a social awareness that has just as important a place in business life as it does in private life.

Good business depends on good manners because they are flattering and make other people feel good, which in turn inspires trust, confidence, and a desire to do business.

When you meet a boor, you remember the boorishness. When you meet good manners, you remember the man.

Meetings

Do you have so many meetings that you can't get on with your work?

Meetings often take up the bulk of a working day, yet they are usually regarded at best as an unwelcome distraction or at worst as a waste of time.

The most common reason is that the meeting is called as the answer to a problem that no one is willing to solve, not as a way of finding the answer.

No meeting can solve anything by its very existence. It is a meeting of people who have taken upon themselves the collective responsibility for reaching a decision. But this needs organizing, so the role of chairman is crucial.

It must be clear at the outset what the meeting is for. The agenda must outline the stages of the discussion, and the chairman must lead the group through these stages, allowing each person his say *in as short a time as possible*.

Long meetings have within them the root of their own inefficiency. People get tired, cease to care, opt for the decision that will lead to a speedy end, and leave grossly dissatisfied.

Short meetings and decisive chairmanship sharpen both the mind and the performance. They produce decisions which people have the dynamism, engendered by the meeting itself, to work on.

Meetings matter, but to work they must be made to work.

Minutes

Should minutes live up to their name?

Minutes should reflect and record the outcome of a meeting and the decisions reached, not the process of arriving at it.

How often have you been bored by a meeting, only to find the minutes even worse? Why record inconclusive discussions on paper so that people can relive their frustrations?

Meetings and their minutes must lead to action, and all minutes should aim to make the best of even the worst meeting. It is surprising how pleased and motivated people become when they read minutes that reflect the best and most productive aspects of the meeting they attended.

Minutes must confirm action agreed, and who is to carry it out. All action points must be named, and if possible timed. Not only who is to do it, but by when.

At the next meeting the reading of the minutes should not be the approval of a historical record, but a questioning of whether the agreed action has been carried out. If it has not, matters arising must consider further action.

Don't let minutes record historical minutiae, make them into an action plan that people can use for the future.

Motivation

Have you ever asked what really motivates you?

There is much talk of motivating others, much analysis of hierarchies of needs at different times of life, and a general consensus that money is not a motivator. But we rarely sit back to review what motivates us, and decide how we might pass on the same motive force to others.

The most powerful motivators, whatever the behavioural psychologists say, are enjoyment of the job you are doing, being told that you doing it well, a sense of achievement, and the confidence that comes from success.

If these motivate you, are you certain that you are doing enough to motivate your staff in the same way?

All too often the importance of motivation is discussed, at tedious length, but very little is done about it. Motivation is not just in the mind, it is the result of personal contact, of personal encouragement, of personal success, and above all of making sure that everyone feels important.

Those who feel unimportant because they are ignored are always demotivated. If you want your company to grow and succeed, everyone deserves your attention.

To be noticed and encouraged is to be motivated. It's what you want. It's what everyone wants.

No

How positive is your negative?

A thoughtless answer 'No' to a well thought out and researched question, is far more discouraging than you might think, simply because you didn't.

It is often easier to say 'No': it involves no commitment, no change, no action and no risk of things going wrong. But are you that sort of manager?

To answer 'No' puts you on the line just as firmly as a 'Yes'. It argues a decision, a policy and a commitment that is the opposite of the person making the request or proposal. Do you want your negative knee-jerk to be interpreted in this way? Not if you want to continue to motivate your staff.

There is no reason why you should not say 'No'. It is often the right answer. But give your staff the benefit of knowing why. You probably know far more about the issue than they do, so share your knowledge with them. They will appreciate you for it, and will be able to use what you tell them to work more constructively within the guidelines you lay down.

Let a 'No' be something on which your staff can build positively.

Notice-boards

When did you last look at your company notice-board?

When you do you will probably find that the more notices
there are on it, the more out of date most of them are, and
the less information of any value it contains.

Decide what information you want disseminated on a
public notice-board — for example, union announcements,
health and safety regulations, staff news, company
progress, social events — and then ensure that the notice-
board is placed where *everyone* will read it. What's the
point of a public notice board that is seen only by those on
that particular floor or who use that particular entrance.
Don't you owe it to your staff to make public notices public?

Above all, keep it up to date. The tatty out-of-date
announcements that infest most notice-boards are the best
reason of all for never sparing the notice-board a glance
even if you pass it every day.

But be careful of your public. Don't put on it company
information that you would not want the casual visitor to
see. Even if your staff ignore all notices, you can be sure
your customers and your competitors will read every word.
Notice-boards are there to be noticed — make sure they
are by making them worth reading.

Objectives

How can you get there if you don't know where you are going?

Objectives have become a management cliché that does them less than justice. So concerned are some managers to be seen to have them that they plan first and define the objectives afterwards. But would you decide to go to Aberdeen when you arrived there?

People need and deserve a sense of direction and a sense of purpose. Whatever they may say, floating through the day waiting for a chance wind to fill out the sails of their job description is not a comfortable way of working.

Forget the portentous word and simply ask your staff to help you answer the question 'Where do we *want* to go?' To ask 'Where are we going?' suggests impotence in the face of outside events, and complete lack of control. It is important that you and your staff are in control and have made a decision *together* about your corporate destination. Once you've done that you'll find that working together towards that objective is automatic.

You can't go to two places at once, so don't fool yourself that multi-objectives are the sign of a true manager.

Two objectives are one too many.

Observation

Do your staff feel you watch them or notice them?

It is easy to ignore what you see every day, and one of the greatest personal crimes is to allow this to happen to people.

You have a responsibility to see your staff as often as you can, not in the sense of meeting them formally, but actually looking at them to take in expressions, demeanour, and that air of excitement, enthusiasm, anxiety or depression.

Looking at your staff afresh each day will help you to gauge morale, and ensure that you put in an appropriate word of encouragement or concern as necessary. This in turn will make people feel noticed, and make you seem more approachable.

But watching people is the opposite. It is threatening, saps initiative, makes people self-conscious and unproductive, and makes you appear critical rather than supportive.

Be seen to see people for what they really are.

Open-plan

Does your open-plan office encourage openness or paranoia?

Open-plan offices require a special type of personal decorum and concern that is usually quite natural but is occasionally forgotten, with unfortunate results.

People are very conscious of territory and want to make a particular space their own. This is as true in an open-plan office as it is in a closed office or at home. Do not allow a corporate view of what is and is not acceptable in the office destroy individuality. Encourage plants, pictures, ornaments at each desk or work station. Arrange the office flexibly, avoiding rigid lines, squared-off desks, or perfect symmetry. Let your open plan be open *and* interesting.

Once inside their space, people are right to treat it as their own and hold conversations, on the telephone or face to face, as if there was no one else around. Respect this privacy. It is a cardinal rule that conversations overheard are not commented on. To break this rule is tc destroy the whole working fabric.

At the same time you must provide a room where staff can hold private conversations. Space is frequently at a premium but it is a false economy to deprive your staff of this.

Look at the arrangement of your open-plan offices and ask yourself whether you would enjoy working there. If the answer is 'No', do whatever is required to change that to a 'Yes'.

Patronage

Is patronage in your company good, bad or indifferent?

There are three sorts of patronage, two good and one bad, and it's important to be aware of all of them.

A condescending or patronizing attitude to your staff or customers is universally bad and must be avoided at all costs. It suggests an insufferable superiority that will win no friends or business.

On the other hand you want to encourage your customers to patronize you in the best sense of giving you their custom and support.

In the same way you may want to act as a patron supporter or mentor of a particular member of staff whom you would like to encourage and help to take on greater responsibility in the future.

Success comes from fostering patronage without patronizing.

People

Do you address memos by title or name?

Much depends on the existing culture of your organization, some require the formality of Mr and Mrs, others the aridity of Marketing or Production Manager, others the humanity of David or Sarah.

If the culture you work in is formal or arid, ask yourself why and how it helps you as a company to perform better. There are few arguments that can actually justify such blatant and rude distancing of your staff.

Informality is not threatening. The world does not collapse with the use of a first name.

Your staff are people. It is extraordinary that such a truism needs to be stated at all, but there are those who appear to make it their business to ignore this. They hide behind titles or formal modes of address which highlights their inability to relate to others on a human level. If you keep others at arms' length, what can you expect them to do for you?

If your staff are distant, how much further away must your customers be. They are people too.

Performance

Do you measure performance or just applaud it?

Not only does everyone need to know where you and they are going, they also need to know how well they are doing along the way.

To wait until the end of the year and congratulate everyone for meeting or exceeding your targets is vital, but not enough. Your staff must be told weekly or monthly how good their performance has been. So don't hide your production, sales or profit figures, share them, and above all explain them.

Many people fall into the trap of thinking that just to pass on bald figures is sufficient to let everyone know how well you are doing. It isn't.

Figures that are clear to you can be a complete mystery to those less closely involved, and it is often very difficult for your staff to understand where *they* are in all the numbers.

Explain how your staff's personal performance has contributed to the present position of the company. Make them feel involved and they will have an immediate way of measuring their own performance.

Express all measures of performance in human terms. Make people see that they affect the company's results by what they do, not just the hours they put in.

Just doing your job is not a measure of performance. It's results that matter. They get the applause.

Personal problems

Are personal problems a problem?

If your attitude to your company and your staff is so single-minded that anything that is not company focused is an intrusion, you have a personal problem of your own.

None of us can lead completely compartmentalized lives, and there will be times when private problems loom large. You must recognize this in others and be prepared to spend time, if invited, to help sort things out. This is always time well spent if you value your staff, and want them to return to peak performance as soon as possible.

But don't think that as a manager you can solve every problem. Have the humility to admit when you are out of your depth, and try to find someone better qualified or more experienced who can help you.

Many problems cease to be a problem at all once they are discussed, so the first step is to encourage people to talk. But there are some problems that everyone, but one, recognizes, and no one is prepared to talk about. These range from body odour and bad breath to drink and drugs. Never fight shy of these. Personal smells are easy to deal with, though a great deal of tact is required. Excessive drinking or a suspected drugs problem is much more serious, and here you may well need professional help, but to begin with it must be you who brings the problem out into the open. Never easy but you must do it.

You owe it to your staff not to let their problems get on top of them.

Praise

Do you expect praise for doing your job?

There are a few who still think that if you do what you are paid to do, you have no right to expect any other reward. But they are often the one group who cannot tolerate being treated in that way themselves.

Everyone wants to be recognized for what they are and what they do, and a word of praise is the greatest encouragement of all.

It need only be a word here or a word there. Lavish encomiums are as out of place as complete silence.

Praise is such an important factor in any manager's dealings with his staff, that you should try to praise, encourage or congratulate someone for something, big or small, every day. And if you can't seem them personally, take the trouble to write them a short note. This often carries even more weight than a quick word in the corridor.

Praise good performance and it will get better.

Private affairs

How public is the private life of your staff?

Some people are able to maintain a level of privacy that makes them an enigma outside their work. Others expose their families, friends, and infatuations to public gaze, wearing their whole life on their sleeve.

There are two kinds of problem here. The intensely private person may need the sharing that his or her colleagues can give, but may be unable to invite it, and would certainly resent an intrusive enquiry. The extrovert opposite may alienate his or her colleagues by an endless recital of personal trivia.

There is little you can do about either of these except be aware that they exist, and try to achieve the happy mean between the two yourself.

Of greater danger is the affair that has to be kept private from some one person or group, be it wife, husband or colleagues. This secrecy can have an insidious effect on those involved and on those who get to know.

You can't legislate against mutual attraction, but you can and should advise against affairs between managers and staff, and avoid all such entanglements yourself, no matter how mutually desirable.

Just like every product, every affair has a life cycle. Growth is exciting and stimulating, but all affairs reach a plateau, and then decline.

No amount of mature objectivity about the realities of the relationship can prepare either side for the problems that may accompany working beside each other as separate exposed selves without titillation or *frisson*.

Think of the end of the affair at the beginning and you may not start.

Promises

Does your encouragement ever promise more than you intend?

Ambition is not an attribute confined to those labelled ambitious. Everyone has ambitions, and everyone looks for signs that these ambitions will be realized. Unfortunately, personal aspirations often operate in a much shorter time-scale than is realistically possible, which means that hints are interpreted as sure signs, and suggestions as promises.

There is a danger therefore that in encouraging people, and in singling them out for special attention, you may inadvertently lead them to expect more than you are prepared to deliver.

This is particularly the case when you are dangling the carrot of future opportunity or possible promotion. It's very easy to do: the casual mention that in a year or so 'things may change . . . the company is expanding . . . I won't be in this seat for ever . . . we'll certainly be looking for people like you to take on new roles . . .' and so on.

Most people accept this at face value and find it encouraging and flattering, but are fully aware that there is a long way to go before any such suggestion becomes a reality. Others, more naive, read far too much between the lines, and see promotion just around the corner. Then when the job they thought was theirs goes elsewhere they lose their ambition, their competitive edge, and are bitterly disappointed.

Promise only what you know you will deliver and what you know your candidate can handle. If you don't, he'll lose his promise.

Redundancy

Is redundancy an end or a beginning?

In recent years, redundancy has been the commonplace of so many news bulletins that its harsh reality has been softened.

Making people redundant is never easy, and every manager should feel it a sign of failure that he has allowed things to reach this point. But blaming oneself is not the answer. If companies are to remain healthy and have a chance of future growth, redundancies are often the only answer, but to make people redundant carries with it obligations, both personal and financial.

Your staff have been important to you, and this importance as people does not stop on the day redundancies are announced. The redundancy package must be negotiated with care and sensitivity on both sides, not allowing the resentment of the one or the misfortunes of the other to cloud objectivity.

Of greater importance is the counselling that must go with redundancy, the genuine effort that is required to help your former staff find other jobs. For this you may need to use consultants from outside, but don't shy away from this, their contribution may be invaluable.

Redundancies in your company should herald a new beginning, not a final disaster, and it is your responsibility to ensure that those you make redundant look on it and use it as a new beginning for themselves.

Your staff may feel they owe you nothing when you say they have to go, but you owe them a great deal.

Rejection

Do you have a formula for rejection letters?

The way you reject people says as much about you and your company as the way you recruit and interview them.

Candidates who have taken the time and trouble to apply, prepare their curriculum vitae, complete an application form, research your company, and attend one or more interviews, deserve more than a standard rejection letter. It only takes one sentence to make such letter personal. Why begrudge your candidates that?

A formula rejection letter is bad, but one that arrives weeks after the interview is worse. All candidates are anxious to know whether they have been successful or not. You are naturally concentrating on your shortlist of real possibilities, but don't let that make you forget the feelings and hopes of all the others. As soon as you know they are not in the running, write and tell them. If you are reluctant to do that until your shortlist interviews are complete, at least write to explain the situation. You lose nothing by doing this and gain much goodwill.

When the final selection has been made, make a special effort to write a personal and encouraging letter to those who are unsuccessful with minimum delay. If you can telephone them first so much the better. It may be difficult but your shortlist deserves no less.

You will earn nothing but thanks and respect for making rejection as pleasant as possible.

Reports

Do you write reports to be read or just filed?

There is an art to report writing, but because reports are usually a chore that has to be completed when there are a thousand other things clamouring for attention, few people give them the creative attention they deserve.

Remember that reports are for other people to read and use. If your reports are useless because they are unreadable, you are not doing yourself justice and you are certainly letting down your colleagues who need your report to do their job better.

Reports should be concise, to the point, jargon free, and sound as if they are written by a human being. If you are in doubt about the quality and effectiveness of your own, read them out loud, for as long as you can bear it.

Reports must also develop an argument, and lead to action. The objective of the report and a summary of the conclusions should appear at the beginning with clear pointers to the action required. Those who wish can then delve into the body of the report for your supporting argument, but if you think no one will want to, why include this in your report at all?

Don't indulge yourself in your reports. They are written for others, not you.

Reprimands

How much rancour do your reprimands raise?

If you feel you need to reprimand someone, always give yourself time to work out what you are going to say, how you are going to say it, and what changes you expect in the future.

A reprimand in the heat of the moment sounds angry, and generates anger not action in response.

It is not easy or pleasant to tell someone that they have done something wrong. But simply bawling them out is not the answer. Find a time and place where you can discuss the issue with them in private. To reprimand people in front of their colleagues or subordinates is unpardonable.

You need to take time to work out why they have acted like this. Is it lack of knowledge about the aims of the company, lack of training, lack of respect for their manager (and that may be you), lack of enthusiasm for the job they are doing, problems with colleagues, problems at home, illness? Any of these reasons could lie behind what at first sight seems to be an inexcusable lapse, and it is your responsibility to find out which.

Then talk on the basis of solving the root cause of the problem, rather than attacking its outward signs. That way your discussion should lead to positive improvement.

If there is no excuse, and performance is genuinely poor, you have no alternative but to take the more drastic step of a formal warning which may ultimately lead to dismissal. This needs even more careful thought and planning, as you must be sure of your facts and willing and able to pursue the matter to the bitter end if necessary.

Just because reprimands are unpleasant, don't rush them. The longer you take, the better they will be.

Signatures

How much weight does your signature carry?

Not a day goes by without your signature being required on something — letters, cheques, approvals, authorizations, orders, contracts — often in conjunction with one or two others.

Signatures on letters must be legible, anything else is an insult. Decide whether you need your title to make it clear who you are. Don't repeat the name of your company. This is old-fashioned and unnecessary.

Do you allow your secretary to sign in her own right, or is she always signing on your behalf? If she has written the letter in your absence, is there any reason why she should not phrase it accordingly and sign it herself?

Think about all those dual and triple authorizations where your signature is one of many. What does that really say about the hierarchy and authority levels in your company? Does it reflect a lack of trust, the inability of managers to delegate, or the naive view that signing equals involvement and control when it means exactly the opposite?

Names and how they are used are important. Don't let people feel they are just rubber stamps. Signatures must carry authority.

Smoking

Do you tolerate, discourage or ignore smoking?

The miasma hanging at head height in an ill-ventilated conference room at the end of the day is enough to drive even the hardened smoker to question his habit. But it is a habit that should be questioned more regularly than the annual sales conference.

If theatres, cinemas, and London Underground can adopt a clear policy on smoking without an outcry at the erosion of civil liberties, why cannot companies take an equally firm line?

That is not to say that smoking should necessarily be banned on company premises (though a non-smoking recruitment policy could be a start), but there is a standard of behaviour that should be the norm. Encourage people to ask others' permission before they light up. At the start of a meeting take a consensus on whether smoking is acceptable. In return, provide a room or rooms where smoking is always permissible, and where non-smokers have no right to complain.

Smokers have a responsibility to think about others' comfort, relaxation and sense of well-being as much as their own.

Strengths

Can you list the strengths of your senior members of staff?

Strengths are not just technical and professional skills that can be measured by practical tests, examinations or observation. Important as these skills are, they are the minimum required for the job, and are not necessarily remarkable.

The strengths you need to look out for are more intangible:

- the ability to work under stress;
- the dynamism that gets things done;
- the breadth of vision that sees the present task in a longer-term context;
- the ability to get on with others and motivate them by example;
- the willingness to accept criticism, and humility to acknowledge when it is deserved;
- ambition that is self-motivating yet realistic;
- the determination to fight for things that matter.

These strengths appear over time, and must be recognized for their oustanding value over and above the professional skills that accompany them.

Professional skills can often be bought off the shelf, or developed by careful training. Human skills are innate. They may be nurtured and encouraged, but are not easily implanted if they are completely absent.

The art of good management is to build on the strengths of your staff as people, not just as job holders.

Success

Do you talk about success or just enjoy it?

Everyone in your company deserves to share in the success that they have *all* achieved. A large order is not just a sales success. A deadline met is not just a production success. An increase in market share is not just a marketing success. A leap in profits is not just a success for the shareholders. Every member of staff is involved in these successes, and they have the right to be told about them as a recognition of their particular contribution.

So spread the word. Tell people that you are doing well. Let your staff see that you are pleased, and encourage them to share in your pleasure.

A success story binds staff together and motivates them. They feel proud to be part of it, and rightly so, and this gives them a new and inspiring confidence when dealing with customers. Suddenly, talking about your products and services is exciting. It's not just sales talk, it's real talk, and the difference is always noticeable.

Talk about success, and everyone enjoys it, including your customers.

Tact

Can you recognize tact only by its absence?

It is easy to recall our own or other people's lack of tact: inept words at the wrong time, thoughtless criticism, flippancy about a painful event, casual, dismissive comment about something intensely personal and important.

We remember our own tactlessness with a shudder, and other people's with anger, resentment, or distaste, but we have the greatest difficulty in guaranteeing that we will never make the same mistake again.

Tact depends on an instinctive sensitivity to situations and people's feelings that leads you naturally to say the right thing.

Sensitivity works in two ways, outward and inward. Outward it is a strength. You want to get the best out of people, and to do that you must avoid alienating them by some thoughtless remark that you will regret and they will remember long after. Inward sensitivity may seem a weakness which tact panders to. Yet it is through an awareness of these so-called weaknesses that you build a strong team.

Lack of tact is the mark of a dictator. Tact is the attribute of a manager.

Talking

Is talking to people your first or last resort?

There are those who believe that a piece of paper is the starting point of all action, and spend long hours writing memos and letters to set up meetings, establish common ground for discussions, or argue points at tedious length.

All of this distances managers from the people who are making things happen, which they are not. If they spoke to people, they would.

Talking to people is a vital part of good management, but its advantages are often ignored. Talking is direct, flexible, guarantees an immediate exchange of views, is supported by eye contact and body language, and allows people to be people.

But some people are afraid of the very things that make talking so valuable, and therefore hide behind paper, little realizing that this merely exposes their human weakness.

Make contact and talk *first*. Confirm what has been agreed (not what has been said) on paper. Everyone then has a record on which to base future action without having to rely on fallible memory. What they will remember is the personal contact.

If you can manage to talk, you can manage people.

Teams

Do you talk about team-work without any teams?

Just because you all have the same objectives does not mean you are a team. Teams are groups of people with different yet complementary skills whose effectiveness as a whole is greater than the effectiveness of any one individual.

It is your job as a manager to identify the skills necessary in any team, and build it accordingly. Teams have to be built, they do not create themselves.

You will need people who

- are naturally creative
- turn creativity into a coherent plan
- tie up loose ends
- can see the gaps others ignore
- work out the resources required
- get the job done
- monitor progress and check on quality

and pulling all these together you must have a project or team leader.

Team building is a complicated process and must be handled with care. An excess or lack of any key skill can put a project, department, or a whole company in jeopardy.

To build a good team you must know people well. The way your staff complement each other is just as important as what they do.

Don't forget that you are a part of a team. Who do you need to complement you?

Thanks

How many of your staff think they have a thankless job?

A thankless job is one that seems to have no point to it, one that no one cares about or recognizes: it doesn't matter, and if you are doing it, you don't matter.

If any one of your staff feels like that, they won't be your staff for very long.

Your staff must have a sense of purpose, must know why they do what they are paid to do, must see how their work contributes to your department or company objectives, must feel that they matter.

And you achieve all that by thanking them.

A quick word of thanks works wonders. It shows that you care, and have taken the time to recognize what other people are doing, and the more mundane their work, the more important this is.

If the job is of particular importance or has been done outstandingly well, a short written word of thanks is even better.

Saying thank-you is a great motivator. It makes people pleased and thankful to be working with you and for you.

Threats

Do threats work?

Threatening people with dire consequences if they don't perform well may appear to produce results, but you can never tell if the results would have been the same, or even better, without the threat.

Threats are a cheap shortcut to getting things done, and should therefore be looked on as a blunt and unsatisfactory weapon, not a management skill. They destroy respect, demotivate, and are only a short-term expedient. People under threat perform out of fear, not because they want to. Long-term success depends on people driving themselves towards an objective they clearly understand and can identify with. They should not need to be driven.

External threats from competitors or changes in the market should have the opposite effect. No one is imposing these on you against your will. They are the hard facts of business life, and if you don't respond to them the consequences will indeed be dire.

No one should set any store by personal threats, but make sure your staff work towards minimizing threats from outside, they are the ones that should make you want to work.

Time

Do you keep time, manage time, or make time?

Being on time for appointments should be an automatic part of any manager's behaviour, and he should expect his staff to emulate him. But being over-zealous about the minutiae of daily time-keeping may suggest a lack of trust and wrong priorities, particularly if your staff are naturally hard working and dedicated.

Managing your own time is more complex, and never as straightforward as the time management experts would have you believe. It requires careful organization, a clear awareness of your priorities, and the ability to step back from daily or hourly pressures and put everything into a more relaxed and longer-term perspective.

The most important and frequently ignored element in all time management is making time for your staff. They must be confident that if they want to see you you will find time for them. Not just a grudging five minutes, but as long as they really need. Don't let them feel that even though you appear to be listening, your mind is elsewhere, and that you can't wait to get back to whatever you were doing before they arrived. Cultivate the habit of devoting yourself to them single-mindedly, as if they are the most important event in your whole day, because that is what you may be to them. Think how you feel if someone treats you in a superficial manner.

Your use of time must never be self-indulgent. As a manager it's not your time that matters, but your time for other people.

Training

Is training just a matter of sending people on courses?

Do your managers measure their training by the number of courses they have attended and feel resentful if they have not been 'away on a course' for some time?

How often do you hear anyone talking about what they learned on a course, or what they can do now that they could not do or did worse before?

Training is a continual building on people's strengths, preparing them for opportunities that lie ahead. You want your staff to grow in their jobs and take on new responsibilities, and you owe it to them to work out a comprehensive training programme that will do this.

You also want your staff to serve your customers better.

Do your staff understand that customers and clients matter, that politeness, courtesy and anticipating the needs of others all pay real dividends? If not, they must be trained to understand.

This is the one kind of training that should always be conducted in-house, where you can tailor the course to particular and individual needs.

Training in company courtesy is training for the future with the customer in mind.

Unpleasantness

Do you avoid unpleasantness at all costs?

No matter how concerned about people you are, nor how strong the cult of courtesy is in your company, you will not work each and every day in perfect harmony, with no friction or personal antagonism.

There will always be tension between people with varying skills from different disciplines who are determined to succeed. This creative tension will sometimes flare up into displays of temper, prolonged rows, or open warfare.

This kind of unpleasantness is more worrying by its absence than its presence, and should not be crushed or avoided. There are times when people need to let off steam. To bottle up their feelings causes more problems than a sudden explosion.

The people to watch however are those who regard it as a virtue to be continually unpleasant and hostile to others. Often this behaviour has more to do with their own personal inadequacies and the pressure they work under, than the activity of their colleagues. In such cases it is not the unpleasantness itself that needs to be addressed, but the root cause.

There will also be situations in which you as a manager have to take difficult and unpleasant decisions about people for their own good and the good of the company. It is this kind of unpleasantness that you cannot afford to avoid.

To avoid an unpleasant decision is managerial cowardice, and will in the end cost far more than short-term pain.

Untidiness

Does untidiness concern you?

If you believe that the world is divided between those who are naturally tidy and those who are not, you probably believe there is nothing you can do about it. But others do not necessarily think the same way.

The environment in which people work is important to their sense of well-being and enjoyment. It is up to you to make sure of this by imposing (and it may well be an imposition on some) the highest standards of tidiness. Don't do this just for the sake of appearances. Do it because it breeds an attitude of pragmatic care and concern that is important in all business dealings.

When you work in the same place day after day, it is very easy to become blind to untidy or slipshod organization. There has to be one person at least who looks at the place with the objective and critical eye of an outsider. That person is probably you.

Untidiness does not just concern inanimate objects, it concerns people. It reflects their attitudes to their work and their attitude to others.

Ask yourself how your customers will react to an untidy office, reception area, or personal appearance. Will they want to do business with you?

Vacancy

Is a vacancy a job for someone or someone for a job?

When somebody leaves your company, do you begin the recruitment of a successor immediately, or do you pause to review the need for the appointment, and the type of person you require?

A vacancy is not just a job not being done, it is a gap that can be described in precise human terms. It is this description that must be the strongest influence throughout your recruitment. So don't rush into recruitment without a clear picture of whom you want.

Applicants invest a large amount of time and energy applying to you and attending interviews. It is a waste of their time and yours if you don't really know what you are looking for.

Equally bad is to change the job specification once the first interviews have been completed, or to go through the whole process and decide that you do not wish to make the appointment at all. If you do that, your candidates have every right to feel irritated and annoyed, and if you want to talk to them again, they'll probably turn you down.

Who would want to work for a company that did not know its own mind?

Don't forget that vacancies have to be filled by people.

Visibility

Do your staff see you regularly?

Successful chief executives all set great store by being seen by their staff. Regular trips up and down the country to visit branches, shops and factories are an essential feature of their management style, and a contributor to their success. No ivory tower management for them. They want to meet and talk to the people on whom they depend.

If the men and women in charge of the largest organizations do it because they believe it works, why don't you?

Human contact is part of good management, but it is up to you to make that contact first. People will not communicate with you unless you communicate with them, and to do that they must see you.

Set aside a time, every day if possible, when you walk around, not on a tour of inspection, but in a relaxed manner that gives you a chance to talk to people. The information you pass on will soon reach everyone, and the information you receive will ensure that you are in close touch with what people feel.

If people see you putting courteous communication into practice they will follow your example.

Weaknesses

Are you positive about your weaknesses?

No body and no company is perfect, but few are willing to admit there is room for improvement.

The drive for success, whether personal or corporate, pressurizes people to cover up their deficiencies in the hope that if all comes right in the end their particular weaknesses will not matter. But there is always a next time.

Concern for people involves helping them, in an unthreatening manner, to identify those weaknesses and look for ways in which they can be strengthened. You will need to decide whether this is best done through formal counselling, a training programme, or via an informal chat over a beer.

Asking people to list their weaknesses is a first step, but do this as part of an appraisal exercise, not cold, and always alongside their strengths. You can then match the one with the other, and help people to see their weaknesses in a positive light. You may even be able to persuade them that what they regard as a weakness is nothing of the sort.

Encourage everyone to be positive about their weaknesses, and what they can do about them.

A weakness is a reason for action, not a cover-up.

You and your customers

Body language

Does your body language say things you would rather keep to yourself?

All managers, representatives, and others in face-to-face contact with staff or customers, are taught to watch the tell-tale body language of the person they are dealing with.

Those involuntary signs of irritation, boredom, fear, surprise, anxiety, pleasure, or triumph can tell you a great deal, and give you a vital negotiating advantage.

But don't forget that the person you are talking to is watching *you* in exactly the same way.

Don't let your body language suggest discourtesies of boredom, condescension, impatience, or amusement that will cause others to remember you, and therefore your company, in a bad or ungenerous way.

How can you be sure about this?

Find a friend and ask.

Bureaucracy

Are your company systems human?

To your customers your company must have a human face, so encourage them to write to or telephone a name, not an impersonal department, or worse still a department number.

Encourage the whole company to adopt a personal style when dealing with customers, and never let the systems you use come between you and the human touch.

At the same time make sure that the internal face of the company is equally human.

Keep impersonal forms to the minimum, address memoranda by name, preferably first in full (not initials) and surname, not just job title, and if your company culture allows use first names in face-to-face contact at all levels.

This does not lead to lax, undisciplined hedonism as some fear, but introduces a warmth and humanity into business practice that ultimately finds its way to the customer.

If you make sure that all your systems are people centred, then the systems will serve you, not the other way round, which is bureaucracy gone mad.

Complacency

Is the way things are the way they will always be?

The combination of a successful business and efficient systems can be fatal. It breeds complacency.

Complacency produces an attitude of mind that says, 'It's all going so well, I don't need to worry'.

Thinking you don't need to worry makes you careless and care less.

You are careless about the future, and don't see the danger signals of market decline, competitor pressure, or customer indifference.

You care less about your customers because you believe they need you more than you need them.

If you don't care about these things, you will soon lose your edge, and you'll lose it first through your customers.

Your customers want to feel that you care about them. If you are so self-satisfied that customers are an irritant, then you deserve all the failure you will certainly get.

Have the courtesy to care about your customers and you will never be complacent, because though your customers are satisfied, you will never be.

Computers

Do you allow your computers to write letters?

The answer is obviously no. But when did you last read the letters that are sent out automatically by your computer?

If you have not done so recently, or worse still ever, you are guilty of one of the most common failings. You have ignored 'standard' or 'form' letters just because they are a formula, but you have forgotten that these letters go to more people than perhaps any other type of correspondence in your company. Don't they deserve an appropriate amount of attention?

The days when it was easy to recognize computer-generated letters, from typeface, layout or paper, are now gone. Laser printers give letters the quality and authority of printed text. It is therefore an even greater crime if such letters lack both.

Don't let your computer staff write important customer contact letters, and don't let them design those letters (or your invoices, dispatch notes or statements) to suit their processing convenience. Design them for the convenience of your customer, and no one else.

If your customers think they are dealing with a computer, they will quickly look for a human being elsewhere.

Contacts

Do you value contacts only if they can help you now?

Address books are full of them. Business card wallets are overflowing with them. Exhibition diaries contain little else. Representatives find it hard to believe that such a vast number produces so little.

Yet contacts are all too often ignored, with serious results. They are the electricity that makes business flow.

It should be a natural part of business courtesy to maintain contact with your contacts, to write to them, briefly, after an exhibition or conference, to send them a Christmas card, to meet them for an occasional drink.

To ignore all but those who can be of immediate benefit to you is not only short-sighted, but rude.

Would you be willing to help someone who treated you with such minimal courtesy?

And don't forget that your contacts give you a unique view of yourself and your company, so how can you afford to ignore them?

Credit control

Is credit control just a matter of making sure that people pay?

No sale is complete until it is paid for, so why do so many companies spend vast amounts on marketing and sales, and then ignore credit control as 'just' an accounting function?

Why are customers courted assiduously when the sale is being made, but treated with sneering disdain afterwards through a series of badly-worded formula letters insisting on immediate payment or dire consequences.

This is not to say that payment does not matter, or that a soft and gentle approach is always the right one. Cash is far more important for the day-to-day health of the company than profits, and customers must be encouraged, cajoled or forced to pay without fear of favour.

What is important is to remember that they are still customers, and you want them to remain so.

Do not divorce your credit control department from your marketing and sales staff. Contact must be frequent and co-operative.

Make sure your marketing and sales staff know all the customers who are currently slow payers *before* any dunning letters go out. The solution may be simple and in the hands of a sales manager.

Let your marketing and sales staff have a say in the composition of all credit control letters.

Make sure your credit control department recognizes that account numbers are *people*, who matter.

Think what sort of approach would encourage *you* to pay.

Customers

Can you answer these questions?

- Who are your customers?
- Where are they?
- What do they buy from you?
- Why do they buy from you?
- What do you think you are giving them?
- How do they rate your products?
- How do they rate your service?
- How often do you communicate with them?
- How do you communicate with them?
- How do they communicate with you?
- What do they think of you?
- When does a customer cease to be of value to you?
- Do all your staff know who your 20 most important customers are?
- In what circumstances would you not put your customers first?
- Can you give one example of customer care and concern from every department in your company?

If you can't answer these questions, ask yourself how your business has survived for so long.

And then ask how much longer it will survive.

Diary

Is the complexity of his diary a measure of a manager's efficiency?

We live in a world of filofaxes, time management systems, business organizers, all of baffling complexity. They all claim to be indispensable aids to modern management, but if the dates can't be seen for the palm fronds of checklists and categorized time bands, these systems are more hindrance than help.

Think back to the days when a diary contained dates, times, and names. Were we any worse off?

A diary is a vital tool because life must be organized weeks, months, if not years ahead, but it is the appointments it contains that matter, not its own organizational characteristics.

Appointments mean people, and people must not be let down. Your diary is the device that ensures that you remember to meet people when you said you would.

This may seem obvious but don't underestimate it. What do you feel if someone forgets, misses, or is late for an appointment made with you?

Appointments are made to be kept, and the first step is to keep them in your diary.

Directors

Do all your staff know the directors of the company by name and function?

All your advertizing and public relations efforts can be reduced to nothing if a customer or client rings to check on the name or function of one of your board, and receives the bored reply, 'Oh, I'll have to ask'.

Or worse, hears his enquiry shouted around the switchboard 'Anyone know the name of the managing director?'

It actually happens.

Telephone your company incognito and find out if it does in yours.

Effort

Do your staff ever give the impression that dealing with other people is rather too much trouble?

Courtesy and good public relations need effort.

Don't ever let your staff suggest on the telephone, in a letter, or when meeting people, that your customers or clients are not worth that effort.

Your staff must show that they are always prepared to put your clients', customers', or visitors' needs first.

Your staff are the company in these situations.

Are they helping or hindering your business by their attitude to others?

Enquiries

Are your staff trained to handle enquiries efficiently, politely, and professionally?

Enquiries are frequently for or about 'the person who looks after the central heating/photocopiers/purchases/payments/complaints/orders/contracts'.

Your customers will not naturally word their enquiries in a way that relates to your company organization. Why should they?

Your staff, particularly reception and switchboard, must be able to route these enquiries quickly to the right person.

It's not always as easy as it sounds. The enquiry may be sensible, but not phrased in a way that shows clearly who they should speak to. Your staff must not try to pin them down to a choice of departments ('well, do you want sales or publicity?') which may mean nothing to them. They must be able to sort this out, without irritation or impatience, to avoid wasting anybody's time.

Train your staff to handle enquiries from overseas with the same care that they give to those from within your country. They must know how to handle differences of language, culture and time zones. A customer is still a customer whether he or she speaks your language well or not.

Knowledge of the company, directors, organization, and staff are all vital here.

Never let the enquirer feel that he or she is an unnecessary irritant to your busy day. If you do, the feeling will certainly be reciprocated, and your company will lose as a result.

The next enquiry may be the prelude to your biggest order of the year.

Enthusiasm

Is enthusiasm one disease you hope your staff won't catch?

Deep in the psyche of many people is the notion that to enjoy yourself is wrong, and to enjoy work is an aberration.

It is for this reason that enthusiasts are frequently avoided, if not actively discouraged by the cold water that is poured on their steaming and bubbling endeavours.

But if your staff are not enjoying what they do there is something seriously wrong, and it is your job to find out what it is.

Once the problems have been unearthed — and it may simply be that you are not enthusiastic enough yourself — it is up to you to foster enthusiasm and a sense of fun.

Lack of enthusiasm is the disease, not the other way round.

Enthusiasm is infectious, and is the one infection you want everyone to catch for the good health of your company.

Exhibitions

When did you last give your staff advice or training on exhibition techniques?

The statement your stand and staff make at exhibitions is critical to your company image, but it is one aspect of business promotion that companies get wrong with appalling regularity.

A badly-organized, ill-conceived display, with badly-organized, ill-informed staff, inadequate printed information, and poor customer reception facilities, sums up a company in one word: 'forgettable'.

Your exhibition must welcome your customers and invite them to learn more. It is there to help them, not as a corporate ego trip.

All this requires hard work before, during and after. Preparation and planning for maximum impact is essential. Meticulous organization is required to ensure that adequate, well-informed and enthusiastic staff are available at all times — and don't forget manning exhibitions is very exhausting. And afterwards, every contact must be followed up.

Don't make an exhibition of yourself at exhibitions.

Fax

Have you ever looked at your own faxed documents?

The convenience and ubiquity of facsimile transmission devices mean that once installed most people rarely give them a second thought.

Yet you worry about your letterheads, and the image created by your receptionist and telephonist. Why should fax be any less important?

Do all your documents go out with a cover page in your house style that is as professionally produced as your letterhead?

Does your fax cover page give full details of your company name, address, telephone and fax number?

Does your fax cover page give the name of the addressee and sender, time of dispatch, and number of pages being sent?

What are the things that irritate you most about other people's faxed material? Are you guilty of the same? How do you know?

Do you know *all* your customers and contacts who have fax, and much more important, do they know you have?

If all this seems irrelevant because you don't have a fax machine, ask yourself why not. The usual answer is, 'We don't need one', but have you ever paused to consider whether *they*, your customers, would find it a convenient, helpful, easy and efficient way to contact you. Don't you owe it to them to install one?

Forms

When did you last fill in one of your own company's forms?

The problem with forms is that we design them to gather information in a convenient and logical sequence in the minimum space, but then never use them ourselves.

The first, and always a classic, is the application form, apparently designed by someone who has never filled one in: maximum space given to health record, languages spoken and military service; minimum space given to past career and interests.

If the curriculum vitae you asked for in the first place gives all this information anyway, why insult people by asking them to put it all down again on your form. If it's so important, why can't you do that?

The secret of all forms is that they are there to be used, for greater efficiency and convenience. So make sure someone in your company uses each form on a trial basis *before* it becomes a company standard.

You will be surprised how often forms waste more time than they save by asking for irrelevant information in an inconvenient way. Do yours?

And don't forget that the forms that were used and were useful last year may need radical revision today.

Freepost

Does all your publicity contain a freepost address or a reply-paid coupon?

The secret of all direct mail or other publicity is to make it as easy as possible for your customers to order from you or ask you for more information.

You want to encourage them. You are trying to win them over. So why should they have to pay to contact you?

Always use freepost, or a reply-paid coupon.

You may not think of this in the context of simple courtesy, but that's exactly what it is.

If they like you, they'll buy from you.

If they don't, they won't.

Gossip

Do your staff gather in public view to chat or gossip?

Not only does this give an impression (however unjustified) of a sloppy firm, but it can also pass on internal information to those who are listening, and they always do.

Internal gossip should remain internal.

It is possible to learn a great deal about the foibles, personal or corporate, of a company by listening to conversations of this kind.

Gossip never presents your company or your staff in a good light.

Grammar

Does good grammar contribute much to your company image?

Maybe not, because it is what people expect, but bad grammar is a form of bad manners, and it does harm.

For a long time the teaching of grammar had a bad press from the educationalists who thought it hindered creativity. Fortunately the backlash is now upon us and there is a move to teach grammar again.

Those who are happy to let their young secretaries correct their grammar may be shocked to discover that letters go out with plural subjects and singular verbs, sentences without subject, or verb, or object, floating phrases with no obvious meaning, wrong gender, wrong possessive, incorrect use of participles, unrelated clauses, confusion of shall and will, should and would. Was your secretary taught to recognize these mistakes?

For many, correcting such things is instinctive and automatic. Others take the view that it is their job to type whatever is written or dictated, whether it makes sense or not. You may not notice this, because you composed it, but the person you are writing to may. What will he think of you when he reads it?

Grammar is too important to leave to others. You must get it right. After all, who is the letter from?

Handwriting

Why do we accept bad handwriting as a fact of life?

If we can't understand what people are saying, we complain. If we can't understand what people write, we complain. If we can't read someone's handwriting, we struggle to decipher as much as we can, and then merely comment that he or she has 'dreadful handwriting'.

There is no excuse for illegible handwriting and if good manners are concerned with being aware of the needs of others, then bad handwriting is bad manners.

For purely practical reasons people must be able to read what you write. You would not accept scrawl from them, so why should they from you?

What would happen if everyone threw away anything they could not read?

Human touch

Do you, or your staff, ever lose the human touch?

We all work under pressure, personal, corporate, or emotional, but we should never allow this to dictate how we deal with customers, clients or other members of the public.

It may be the eightieth enquiry, the twentieth visitor, or the tenth candidate, for *you*. For them it may be the one and only time they are in contact with you.

Everyone must be treated in the same courteous way, never as a cipher.

Remember, and use, your customer's or client's name wherever possible.

No matter how little time you've got, you must give the impression that you have all the time in the world for them.

It's easily said, but it's not often done.

When it is, people remember.

Invoices

When did you last look at your own invoices?

An invoice is not just a document that tells customers what they owe, it contains a mass of other information that your customer must have: product number, description, quantity, price, discount, carriage and packing charges, VAT, date, dispatch date, items to follow, items out of stock, number of invoices making up this order, other information you wish to pass on.

Put yourself in your customer's place and ask, is the information presented in a logical and comprehensive way? Is it obscured by misaligned columns, and abbreviations for which there is no key, and is it therefore meaningless? Do you reproduce out-of-date stock information on your invoices because the computer has not been updated? Is the calculation sequence clear? Is the information about items not available helpful or just irritating? Are payment dates clear?

You and your staff will be quick to notice and exploit any such inadequacies in invoices from your suppliers, so why are you so complacent about your own?

There is no law that says an invoice cannot be a human document. The fact that it is produced by a computer is no excuse. Insert a modicum of humanity, and your customers will notice, and thank you.

Job applications

Do you acknowledge all job applications?

Applications can be a problem if they arrive constantly, or in large numbers, particularly if the majority are of no interest to you.

Do not let lack of interest blind you to the fact that people have taken the time and trouble to write to *you*, and therefore deserve the courtesy of an acknowledgement.

Standardized or formula applications can be acknowledged with a pre-printed card. Others should receive a short, word-processed letter.

If you are involved in a specific recruitment, don't forget that a three-week or three-month time line may be quite acceptable to you, but could be intolerable for your candidates.

Do them the courtesy, in your acknowledgement, of explaining how long the process may take, and when they are likely to hear from you again.

This is the only contact most of these people will have with your company. Their memory of how they are treated may last them a lifetime.

Don't forget that people always talk most about their bad experiences.

Knowledge

Do your staff know what products and services you offer?

The worst public relations fault is the telephonist, receptionist, or anyone else, who does not know what you do, or where you do it, and clearly does not care.

Customer service departments have been known to deny the very existence of an important product line. Telephonists have been known to reject enquiries for a product that was the subject of a current TV and print advertizing campaign.

Make sure that all your staff receive, and read, a company profile, which must be updated regularly.

Make sure that all your staff receive, and read, company product information sheets, catalogues, and other publicity material.

Make sure that all your staff know something about your industry and your standing within it.

Don't forget that anyone who knows so little about your industry that he/she cannot recognize your competitors is a liability.

Talk to your staff about the company and its products or services with pride and enthusiasm. Make people absorb this knowledge by exciting their interest so they are as committed as you are.

Find out if they do know what you want them to know. If they can talk to you, sensibly and with pride, about the company and its products or services, they can talk to others, and that's good.

All your staff are selling in one way or another.

If they have the knowledge, it can only pay dividends. If they don't, you won't.

Lavatories

What image do your lavatories create?

As a visitor, one of the first things you would notice in other companies is the state of their lavatories. It's therefore surprising that it is the one area people often ignore in their own building.

The reason is simple. How often do you use the same lavatories as your visitors?

If you don't, do so today and find out if they match the image created by your receptionist, your reception area, your publicity.

Your expectations must be no lower than your visitor's; and his will be the highest.

Letters

Has the telephone taken over as the main means of communication in your company?

People have long claimed that the art of letterwriting is dead, and looking at the average business letter you would probably agree.

Poor layout, stock phrases, long-windedness, bad punctuation, lack of paragraphs, poor construction, spelling and grammar are all signs that, if the art is not dead, it is certainly moribund.

The look of the letter on the page is the first thing that strikes you, so it pays dividends to ensure that your letters are laid out attractively with wide margins, good spacing, visually centred on the page.

After look and layout comes length. An over-long letter puts people off. When you are dictating don't fall into the trap of saying too much. Brevity and conciseness are the key. Why waste people's time asking them to read more than they have to? Their boredom threshold is possibly even lower than yours.

Look at the letter on the next page. It contains 30 errors. How many can you find? The correct version is on page 107.

If you spotted most of the mistakes, there's every chance you won't make the same ones yourself.

If you didn't, your letters may let you down.

Dear John,

I should like to confirm my telephone conversation with your purchasing superviser yesterday. We agreed in principal that you would send us fourty samples from your new womens' clothing range.

To prevent any customs' embarassment, all boxes must be clearly marked: 'Samples: no comercial value'. Please advice us of your dispatch date, so that we can arrange a waver of import tarifs.

As to your next visit July is preferrable, but I don't anticipate that we will have fulfiled all orders by then.

We are targetting currant promotion on the south east of England, predominately in rural areas, but this season is turning out to be very different to any other I have known. Sales in the first month were negligable, and its now a forgone conclusion that we will have to remail all key accounts in May to insure that neither your lines nor my own stock are left unsalable at the end of the season.

I must consede that, despite my early fears, our customer survey confirms that all your stock should be offerred at full price immediately, with promotion focussing around lifestyle rather than adaptability. Selling at those prices, there must be more money around than I thought.

If this is acceptible, could you telex acknowledgement, confirming who's signature you would like on the order.

Yours sincerly

Mortimor Philpott
Manging Director

106

Dear John,

I should like to confirm my telephone conversation with your purchasing *supervisor* yesterday. We agreed in *principle* that you would send us *forty* samples from your new *women's* clothing range.

To prevent any customs' *embarrassment*, all boxes must be clearly marked: 'Samples: no *commercial* value'. Please *advise* us of your dispatch date, so that we can arrange a *waiver* of import *tariffs*.

As to your next visit July is *preferable*, but I don't *expect* that we will have *fulfilled* all orders by then.

We are *targeting current* promotion on the south east of England, *predominantly* in rural areas, but this season is turning out to be very different *from* any other I have known. Sales in the first month were *negligible*, and *it's* now a *foregone* conclusion that we will have to remail all key accounts in May to *ensure* that neither your lines nor my own stock are left *unsaleable* at the end of the season.

I must *concede* that, despite my early fears, our customer survey confirms that all your stock should be *offered* at full price immediately, with promotion *focusing on* lifestyle rather than adaptability. *If they sell at those prices*, there must be more money around than I thought.

If this is *acceptable*, could you telex acknowledgement, confirming *whose* signature you would like on the order.

Yours *sincerely*

Mortimor Philpott
Managing Director

Market

Do you see your market as segments or people?

Marketing theory, which lays such emphasis on the customer and ways of satisfying his needs, has an uncanny habit of dehumanizing the whole process. It emphasizes target segments, market share, categories of need, price sensitivity, outlets and distribution channels. Where are the people?

The increasing corpus of books on marketing all emphasize that selling and other forms of customer contact are an integral part of the mix, but this emphasis is often diluted by abstractions and analyses that turn marketing into a cold science rather than warm, human art.

Never forget that your market consists of people, like you, who have to be questioned, courted, cajoled, enticed, seduced, rather than simply penetrated.

Your market is not a defenceless victim prey to your aggressive sales campaign.

To buy from you now, and want to buy from you again, your customers must like what you are and what you do for them. Do not allow yourself or your staff to forget this.

Markets are human, and can reject in seconds what it has taken you years to produce.

Messages

Does every member of your staff take messages efficiently?

It is often the simplest of activities that leads to the greatest frustration and harm to your company image.

For example, a client or customer rings up to leave a simple message. The manager concerned is out. His secretary can't be found. Someone unknown (or the switchboard) eventually answers the telephone. He/she reluctantly agrees to take the message. They misunderstand it, and make it quite clear that this is the last thing they want to do, or should be doing.

The client/customer puts the telephone down, furious, and the message is probably not passed on either.

All staff must be ready to take messages at any time, on behalf of their superiors, peers or subordinates, with all the natural skill and courtesy that they themselves would expect from others.

Names

Do you introduce visitors in such a way that both sides remember names?

In the stress of the moment, introductions are often handled perfunctorily as people hurry to get on with the business of the day. This inevitably leads to problems later as everyone can remember what was said, but not who said it.

At the start of formal meetings take introductions slowly, make sure that circulated papers contain the names of the participants and, as chairman, refer to people by name frequently when you speak.

We could do well to adopt the Japanese habit of exchanging business cards on all occasions, both formal and informal. Few people in Japan have any real problem remembering names.

Business cards are an underused and underrated courtesy.

Train your staff, particularly your receptionist and telephonist, to remember *and use* the names of key clients and customers.

Nothing impresses people more than the fact that they are remembered and greeted by name.

Organization

Are all your staff familiar with the organization of your company?

All staff should be given charts that explain your company's staff structure, and its relationship to subsidiaries, branches, and its parent or holding company.

These charts should list people's names as well as their functions, and give the addresses and telephone numbers of the main branches and subsidiaries worldwide.

All staff should be aware of the towns and countries in which you operate.

Ensure that everyone, particularly newcomers, knows who does what, where, and who works for whom. Messages and queries can thus be routed efficiently without going through one or more intermediaries.

Don't forget that a map of where everyone sits in your office is just as important as a map of your branches across the country or around the world.

Normally all this happens as a matter of course.

When it doesn't, the visitor notices.

Public relations

Is public relations something you hire someone else to handle?

Public relations is not a mystique or technique known only to PR experts, adept at handling the media to your advantage. It is a vital part of business life that you yourself must be both aware of and good at.

Public relations covers every facet of communicating with people (not just media people), inside and outside your company. To confine it to the work of consultants, essential as they are in certain fields, is to miss the point of the work they are doing on your behalf.

Great skill is required in helping the public appreciate your company, and you must live up to the expectations that are raised. The success of any public relations activity depends on your skill at treating your customers or clients well. Fail in this, and the best public relations in the world cannot help you. Concentrate on basic and simple courtesies, and the rest will follow almost automatically.

Get your public relations right throughout your company and you will get the right business and get your business right.

Quality

Is getting the job done more important than doing it well?

The relentless pressure of deadlines, delivery dates, sales targets, and the competition, all too often make people forget that if the quality of the product or service suffers there may be fewer and fewer delivery dates, and more and more competition.

Quality is what you promise your customers and if they discover that your promise is vain they will feel cheated. No one likes a cheat.

Quality on the other hand depends on team-work, and the ability of the whole company to think in the same way. It only needs one poor component in thousands, or one unhelpful member of your staff among hundreds, for the whole product or company to be rejected in one person's eyes. He will tell others.

The pursuit of quality forces people to think about the way they work for the benefit of their customer, so don't leave it to experts or consultants. It is something you and your staff must be directly involved in.

Your staff must realize that in the pursuit of quality it is not you who is telling them what is required, it's the customer.

Reception

Does your reception area say what you want it to say about your company?

Reception is where people begin their contact with your company. First impressions are important.

Your receptionist must be well-groomed, polite, informed, and helpful. He/she must be obviously in command of the job, and not flustered by the conflicting demands of visitors, telephone, and telex. He/she must never conduct personal telephone conversations within the hearing of visitors.

The reception area itself must be clean and tidy — not cluttered with datapost deliveries, artwork waiting for a courier, bulk toilet rolls, and that repaired typewriter. No one sees these things but the visitor.

There should be adequate seating for your visitors, access to lavatories, and most important of all a good supply of publicity material, catalogues, and give-aways, which visitors should be encouraged to take with them.

Your products and services must also be displayed prominently, and don't forget to change this display regularly, for the benefit of your own staff, just as much as your visitors.

The reception area must sell your company. Visitors must take away a positive impression of you and your products and services (plus something to jog their memory). They must not just pass through.

Replies

Does the speed of your response to enquiries match the lavishness of your publicity?

There seems to be a law that the more strident the appeals to 'Write now . . .' 'Post today . . .' 'Telephone our hot-line . . .', the longer it takes for the order or request to be dealt with.

When you invite a response (and every piece of publicity should), make sure you reply quickly.

You have excited people's interest, but they will quickly go off the boil if you don't seize the opportunity fast.

It is discourteous, and bad business, to do otherwise.

Don't forget the freepost address, reply-paid coupon, or freephone number.

Don't be guilty of forgetting to include your name and address altogether. It happens.

Publicity is your way of talking to your public. Make sure it becomes a dialogue.

Spelling

Is spelling something you need to worry about?

If you are confident that you have no problem with spelling, there is nothing to worry about. If you are not sure, and expect your secretary to put your letters right if you go wrong, think again. How do you know if she's right?

It is very easy to ignore bad spelling in something you have written. You tend to read what should be there, even if it isn't. But the person to whom you are writing will probably spot a mis-spelled word immediately he opens the letter, and that tells him something about you.

Bad spelling suggests either that you could not be bothered to check the letter (is this symptomatic of your whole attitude to business?), or that you just can't spell (is this an indication of your education and experience?). Your customer can take his choice, and neither is good for you.

Watch out for the common mistakes. Is it -ence or -ance, -ent or -ant, -rr- or -r-, -ie- or -ei-, -ce or -se, 's or s'?

Equally important are technical terms, and names of places, processes and people peculiar to your industry. Get these wrong and your clients and customers have every right to question your business acumen.

Above all you must spell the name of the person you are writing to correctly. A mis-spelled name at the start of a letter destroys its whole impact and your own credibility.

Just think how you feel if people spell *your* name wrongly.

116

Telephone

Do you treat the telephone with the respect it deserves?

The telephone is sometimes the first and often the most important point of contact with your company, and the attention that is paid to it must match this. Are you, or a senior member of your staff, involved in the selection and training of your telephonist? Are you confident that your switchboard staff know all they need to know about your company, its products, services and people? If not, why not?

Make sure your switchboard answers with the full name of the company, or a *recognizable* abbreviation. And never allow your callers to hear the end of your telephonist's conversation first. It happens all too often.

Don't forget the answerphone. Most people do.

The answerphone is just as important a contact with the company as the switchboard. It is usually ignored, and degenerates to an indistinct mumble that gives callers no confidence that their message will actually be listened to, and it often isn't.

People don't like talking to answerphones. Encourage them simply to leave their name, telephone number and the person or department they wish to speak to, and *guarantee* that they will be called back the next day. Check to make sure this happens. Never let your answerphone take calls during normal working-hours, unless you are running the business single-handed. Above all, use a voice for your recorded message that people will enjoy listening to.

Don't let your telephone let you down.

Telex

Do you train people to use your telex?

Telex is a very powerful medium of communication. It is fast and carries hard information, and therefore should not be used casually.

Your staff must be aware of the relative costs of fax and telex, know when to use one and not the other, and know how to make the best use of telex time without sounding excessively curt or using abbreviations or short forms that are more of a hindrance than a help.

Customers can be annoyed just as easily by an ineptly worded telex as they can be by a poor letter, particularly if they are using telex to save time, and your reply wastes it.

You must be sure that your staff can provide an immediate telex answer if required. To delay answering a telex query is unforgiveable. It negates the whole point of using the system. Just think how you would feel.

Lax telex habits can seriously let you down, so train your staff to handle more than just the machine.

Values

Are your values obvious?

People talk confidently about the financial targets of their business, and they use profitability, turnover, return on capital, or share price to measure their success. They are far less open about the ethics of their business, and have great difficulty in measuring their personal code of values.

The ethics of a business concern the way we treat people, and the way they treat us. Is your relationship based on mutual trust and respect, or on doubt and suspicion? Do you seek to gain a business advantage at all costs, irrespective of the personal consequences to others, or do you put people first?

Your scale of values has a direct effect on others, and they will soon learn the terms on which you expect to do business.

Success coupled with high principles earns infinitely more respect than success achieved by other means, if that can be called success.

Some people fight shy of talking about ethics or personal values. There is a fear that to do so exposes a moral streak in their character that others would find as difficult to accept as a religious tract.

It is an inverted hypocrisy to refuse to admit the high principles by which you govern your life.

Admit to your values and you will be surprised how many like-minded people you will find.

Waiting

Do you try to keep people waiting as little as possible?

To keep people waiting is a very common fault, and one of the most irritating.

You wait for replies to letters, you wait for people to answer the telephone, and you are kept waiting long after your appointment time, often without the courtesy of an apology.

You would always expect others to apologize to you for keeping you waiting. Make sure you do the same to them.

It is another memory that lingers long, and reflects on your overall efficiency and quality of business practice.

The fact that other people do it is not an excuse you can use.

Who's where

Do your reception and switchboard staff know who's in your company?

Simple knowledge of the organization and its structure is not enough. It requires a more detailed knowledge of individual movements, work-styles, and support staff.

How often have you waited on the telephone while they are 'trying to find' the person you wish to speak to? To be told, 'He was here a minute ago', is not helpful.

Does that happen in your company?

Take your reception and telephone staff round the building so that they can see where people sit and work in relation to each other. It is not always clear from extension numbers.

Encourage all staff to let their secretary and/or the switchboard and reception know where they are during the day. Explore the cost effectiveness of paging systems if this is not practical.

To find people quickly is a sign of efficiency and courtesy.

'X' factor

Do you encourage your staff to look for that little extra?

Companies, circumstances, markets, and customers are all different, and change constantly, so there is no definitive set of rules for company courtesy.

The items in this book should be the norm in your company, and will be noticed only by their absence. But as far as your customers are concerned it is that *extra* courtesy or demonstration of concern that matters.

It's this extra that marks you out from the competition. That's good news and good business.

Courtesy checklists

All your staff will need to be trained in some aspect of company courtesy.

Every chapter in this book is for them as well as you.

Set up a training programme now to improve the personal and public relations in your company.

To help you do this, there are checklists on the following pages containing 20 company courtesy rules for:

- Managers
- Staff
- Secretaries
- Receptionists
- Telephonists
- Representatives
- Exhibitions.

Give all the relevant staff a copy of these lists, and a copy of this book, and wait for your customers to comment on the improvement.

Remember good public relations start *inside* your company.

Manager's checklist

Twenty company courtesy rules for managers:

1 The way you treat your staff affects the way they treat your customers.

2 Train your staff in good personal relations, using the chapters in the section on 'You and Your Staff'.

3 Train all your staff in good public relations, using the chapters in the section on 'You and Your Customers'.

4 Know your customers.

5 See everything through your customers' eyes, and make improvements for their benefit.

6 Check personally on standards of courtesy and customer care at all levels.

7 Give your staff all the information they need to do their job well.

8- Show your staff how they have contributed to your success.

9 Expose your values.

10 See and be seen.

11 Talk first, then write.

12 Write for future action, not historical record.

13 Know your staff.

14 Build teams, not empires.

15 Praise and thank your staff regularly.

16 Make reprimands and criticism positive.

17 Be prepared to listen.

18 Be prepared to see things from other points of view than your own.

19 Never be complacent.

20 Set a personal example of courtesy and customer care that others can emulate.

Staff checklist

Twenty company courtesy rules for your staff:

1 Learn as much as you can about your company.

2 Prepare a file of company information.

3 Find out how your department contributes to the success of the company.

4 Know who are the key staff in other departments.

5 Ask to see performance statistics for your department. If they are not clear, ask your manager to explain them.

6 If you have a problem, don't be afraid of discussing it with your manager.

7 Look at everything you do through the eyes of your customers or clients.

8 Suggest ways in which your job or department could be changed to serve customers better.

9 Dress with your customers in mind.

10 Remember that when dealing with a customer you are the company.

11 Take telephone messages efficiently and pass them on.

12 Never let your tone of voice on the telephone suggest anything other than helpful concern.

13 Let your job description be a guide, not a strait-jacket.

14 Take criticism positively.

15 Never gossip about the company to outsiders.

16 Talk about success with pride.

17 Don't be ashamed of loyalty or enthusiasm.

18 Be aware of your strengths and weaknesses

19 Work out how you and your colleagues complement each other in the team.

20 Look for ways in which you can provide the extra which your customers or clients will remember.

Secretaries' checklist

Twenty company courtesy rules for secretaries:

1 Find out as much as you can about your company, don't wait to be told.

2 Prepare a file of key company information, and have it to hand at all times.

3 Find out as much as you can about the responsibilities of the person you work for.

4 Recognize and respect his/her priorities and pressures.

5 Organize his/her diary to leave time for regular staff contact.

6 Keep a record of staff birthdays and addresses.

7 Make it clear what kind of dictation and handwritten material helps you most.

8 If you don't understand, ask.

9 Be prepared to make suggestions for improvements.

10 Always respect confidentiality.

11 Check everything for grammar and spelling errors.

12 Remember that layout and presentation are as important as the contents of any letter or report.

13 Know who your main customers or clients are.

14 Know who your main competitors are.

15 Remember the names of your key contacts.

16 Always greet people warmly and by name.

17 Smile when you are speaking on the telephone.

18 Always write down messages.

19 Always apologize if you keep people waiting.

20 Make sure urgent matters are dealt with urgently.

Receptionists' checklist

Twenty company courtesy rules for receptionists:

1 Learn as much as you can about the company you represent to all visitors.

2 Have a file of key company information to hand at all times.

3 Make sure that company publicity material and information is available in reception at all times.

4 Throw away all out-of-date publicity/information material.

5 Encourage visitors to read and take away publicity and information material.

6 Keep the reception area tidy.

7 Get rid of deliveries or dispatch material quickly.

8 Know the names of all the key staff in the company.

9 Make sure you can find people quickly.

10 Know the names of key customers or clients.

11 Remember the names of regular visitors.

12 Always greet people warmly and by name.

13 Smile.

14 Never let your own mood or feelings override good manners.

15 Dress in a way that enhances the image of the company.

16 Never gossip or make personal telephone calls in front of visitors.

17 Discourage staff from using reception as their own meeting place.

18 Find out quickly what people want.

19 Always aim to be as helpful as possible.

20 Always apologize if visitors are kept waiting.

Telephonists' checklist

Twenty company courtesy rules for telephonists:

1 Learn as much as you can about your company.

2 Have a file of key company information to hand at all times.

3 Answer each call with the company name, *and* an appropriate greeting.

4 If the company is known by initials, say these clearly. If this is impossible, give the name in full.

5 Smile when you are speaking.

6 Never let your own mood or feelings show in your voice.

7 Know the names and responsibilities of all the directors in your company.

8 Know the names and titles of all the key staff in your company.

9 Ask to be taken round the building so that you can see where people sit.

10 Make sure you can find people quickly.

11 Don't ask callers to specify a department, ask them what they want, and route accordingly.

12 Know the names of key customers or clients.

13 Remember the names of regular callers, and greet them by name.

14 Never let callers hear the end of your conversation as you answer.

15 Check the quality of your answerphone message, and re-record regularly.

16 Make sure all answerphone messages are passed on without delay.

17 Don't let callers hang on indefinitely.

18 Always apologize if you keep people waiting.

19 Aim to be as helpful as possible at all times.

20 If you are responsible for the telex, answer telex messages with the same speed and courtesy as telephone calls.

Representatives' checklist

Twenty company courtesy rules for representatives:

1 Know your customers.

2 Know your products or services.

3 Relate products and services to customers' needs.

4 Talk about benefits, not specifications.

5 Be prepared to take criticism on your company's behalf.

6 Never criticize other departments to your customers.

7 Talk about successes.

8 Let your customers see that you are there to help them.

9 Always do what you say you are going to do.

10 Keep in touch with all your contacts.

11 Recognize the cumulative value of every sales visit.

12 Remember your customers' names.

13 Greet people warmly and by name.

14 Smile.

15 Leave some publicity material behind at every call.

16 Plan your sales visits to suit your customers.

17 Make appointments, and keep them.

18 Dress with your customers in mind.

19 Know your company as well as its products.

20 Make your pride in your company obvious.

Exhibitions checklist

Twenty company courtesy rules for exhibitions:

1 Decide what you want your exhibition to say, not display.

2 Focus on key products or services.

3 Don't attempt to show everything.

4 Have adequate supplies of publicity and promotion material available.

5 Make your stand welcoming.

6 Don't allow staff to obscure display.

7 Provide refreshments.

8 Never ask 'Can I help you?'

9 Always ask open-ended questions to find out your visitor's particular need or interest.

10 Show how your products or services meet the needs of your visitor.

11 Talk about benefits, not specifications.

12 Take the name and address of every visitor.

13 Don't let any visitor leave your stand empty handed.

14 Look and sound enthusiastic at all times.

15 Provide enough staff to cover the exhibition on a rota basis to reduce fatigue.

16 Make sure all staff have adequate product knowledge.

17 Train all staff to handle visitors courteously.

18 Make the exhibition an event for your customers, not a chore for your staff.

19 Look at your exhibition and your staff through the eyes of your customers, and make improvements accordingly.

20 Follow up every exhibition contact.

Recommended reading

Adair, John, *Effective Leadership*, Gower, 1983.

Bolton, Robert, *People Skills*, Prentice-Hall, 1979.

Bowman, Pat and Ellis, Nigel, *Manual of Public Relations*, Heinemann, 1982.

de Board, Robert, *Counselling People at Work*, Gower, 1983.

de Board, Robert, *Counselling Skills*, Wildwood House, Gower, 1987.

Devery, C., *Working with a Secretary — a manager's guide*, The Industrial Society, 1986.

Freemantle, David, *Superboss — The A–Z of Managing People Successfully*, Gower, 1985.

Gowers, Sir Ernest, *The Complete Plain Words*, revised by Sir Bruce Fraser, Penguin, 1973.

Martin, Peter and Nicholls, John, *Creating a Committed Workforce*, Institute of Personnel Management, 1987.

Reynolds, Helen and Tramel, Mary, *Executive Time Management*, Gower, 1985.

Scott, Bill, *The Skills of Communicating*, Gower, 1986.

Stewart, Dorothy (ed.), *Handbook of Management Skills*, Gower, 1987.